Masters of the Italian Art Song:

word-by-word and poetic translations of the complete songs for voice and piano

by
Timothy LeVan

The Scarecrow Press, Inc.
Metuchen, N.J., & London
1990

British Library Cataloguing-in-Publication data available

Library of Congress Cataloging-in-Publication Data

Masters of the Italian art song : word-by-word and poetic transla-
   tions of the complete songs for voice and piano / by Timothy
LeVan.
      p.   cm.
   Includes indexes.
   ISBN 0-8108-2363-2 (acid-free paper)
   Contents: Bellini -- Donaudy -- Donizetti -- Puccini -- Rossini
-- Tosti -- Verdi.
   1. Songs--Texts. I. LeVan, Timothy, 1961-
ML54.6.M34   1990 <Case>
782.42168'0945--dc20   90-8955

In Memoriam

Joel Thompson

1957-1990

Contents

Acknowledgements

My deepest thanks go to Mary Burgess, Eloisa Richmond, Paul Jordon, to the constant revelations of Peyton Hibbitt, Carmen Savoca and Duane Skrabalak, and all those who have encouraged my ongoing progress in the lifetime discovery of language.

Preface

It is the hope of the author to provide an aid to all students of language by presenting precise word-by-word and poetic translations of the texts of the complete songs for voice and piano of Bellini, Donaudy, Donizetti, Puccini, Rossini, Tosti and Verdi.

The author encourages ongoing thoughtful evaluation of the relative strength, color, explicit and implicit meaning of each word, phrase, sentence and poem. It is his intent to use cognates wherever possible as a learning tool for the English-speaking artist.

Timothy LeVan is a pianist/vocal coach who teaches in the Masters of Opera Degree Program co-sponsored by the Tri-Cities Opera Company and The State University of New York at Binghamton. Previously, he has worked as pianist/vocal coach at the Pittsburgh Opera, the Pittsburgh Chamber Opera, the Ithaca Opera and the C.W. Post Summer Opera. He works with many artists from the Metropolitan Opera, the New York City Opera Companies and travels worldwide as an accompanist.

Mr. LeVan holds a B.F.A. in Piano from Carnegie-Mellon University and has done graduate studies at the University of Lausanne and the Conservatory of Fribourg, Switzerland.

He is currently at work on a partner volume to The Masters of the Italian Art Song, entitled Masters of the French Art Song, featuring the complete songs of Chausson, Debussy, Duparc, Fauré, and Ravel. He has completed an earlier booklet of translations, Twenty-Four Italian Songs with Word-by-Word and Poetic Translations.

Introduction

This text is organized alphabetically, first by composer and second by song title.

Each song text is in a three-line format:

Line 1: The original-language text.

Line 2: A word-by-word, vertically accurate translation in the original word order, i.e.

> Ma crin d'oro ha il mio tesoro....
> But hair of-gold has the my treasure....
> (But my treasure has hair of gold....)

The number of English "words" is consistent with the number of original-language "words", i.e. Sento nel core (three Italian words) is translated as: I-feel in-the heart (three English "words"). Hyphenation is used to accomplish this.

Line 3: A reconstruction of line #2 into more standard English. This line is not a freely poetic translation of the original-language text. Rarely has the author taken the liberty of translating beyond the literal meaning i.e. "crin d'oro" is translated as "hair of-gold," not "blond hair."

This three-line format is designed to help the reader in a translational process from original language, to word-by-word translation, to more standard English translation, and to a final artistic interpretation based upon the reader's knowledge gained from this step-by-step process.

Bellini
Almen se non poss'io
At-least if not can-I

Almen se non poss'io Seguir l'amato bene,
At-least if not can-I Follow the-lover well,
(At least if I cannot follow my well beloved,)

Affetti del cor mio, Seguitelo per me.
Affections of-the heart my, Follow-him for me.
(Affections of my heart, follow him for me.)

Già sempre a lui vicino
Already always to him near
(Already always near him affections of love)

Raccolti amor vi tiene
Gathered-you love you holds
(Gather around and hold him)

E insolito cammino Questo per voi non è.
And unusual pathway This-one for you not is.
(And this is not an unusual pathway for you.)

Bellini
Bella Nice, che d'amore
Beautiful Nice, which of-love

Bella Nice, che d'amore
Beautiful Nice, which of-love
(Beautiful Nice, you gave me the trembling)

Desti il fremito e il desir, ah!
you-Gave the trembling and the desire, ah!
(and desire of love, ah!)

Bella Nice, del mio core Dolce speme e sol sospir,
Beautiful Nice, of-the my heart Sweet hopes and alone sigh,
(Of beautiful Nice my heart has only sweet hopes and sighs,)

Ahi! verrà, nè sì lontano
Oh! it-will-come, neither so far-away
(Oh! it will come,)

Forse a me quel giorno è già,
Perhaps to me that day is already,
(perhaps that day already is not far away,)

Che di morte l'empia mano Il mio stame troncherà.
That of death the-evil hand The my stamina will-shorten.
(When the evil hand of death will shorten my life.)

Quando in grembo al feral nido
When in womb to-the fatal nest
(When in the womb, oh! miserable, I will be)

Peso, ahi! misero, io sarò,
Heavy, oh! miserable, I will-be,
(in the heavy nest of death.)

Deh! deh, rammenta quanto fido Questo cor ognor t'amò.
Oh! oh, recall how-much faithful This heart still you-loved.
(Oh!, oh, remember how much this faithful heart still loved you.)

Sul mio cenere tacente Se tu spargi allora un fior,
On my ashes silent If you scatter then a flower,
(Then if on my silent ashes you scatter a flower,)

Bella Nice, men dolente Dell'avel mi fia l'orror.
Beautiful Nice, less painful Of-the-grave to-me is the-horror.
(Beautiful Nice, less of a horror to me is the painful grave,)

Non ti chiedo che di pianto Venga l'urna mia a bagnar, ah!
Not to-you I-ask that of tears Come the-tomb my to wet, ah!
(I do not ask that you wet my tomb with tears, ah!)

Se sperar potess'io tanto, Vorrei subito spirar.
If to-hope could-I so-much, I-Would-like soon to-expire.
(If I could wish for so much, I would like soon to die.)

Bellini
Dolente immagine di Fille mia
Painful image of Fille my

Dolente immagine di Fille mia,
Painful image of Fille my,
(Painful image of my Fille)

Perchè sì sqallida mi siedi accanto?
Why so miserable to-me you-sit near?
(Why so miserably do you sit near me?)

Che più desideri?
What more wish-you?
(What more do you want?)

Dirotto pianto Io sul tuo cenere versai finor.
Pouring tears I on-the your ashes shedded till-now.
(I have poured my tears on your ashes up till now.)

Temi che immemore de' sacri giuri
You-are-Afraid that forgetful of-the sacred oaths
(Are you afraid that, forgetting our sacred vows,)

Io possa accendermi ad altra face?
I could burn-me to another face?
(I could love another face?)

Ombra di Fillide, riposa in pace;
Shadow of Fillide, rest in peace;
(Shadow of Fillide, rest in peace;)

E inestinguibile l'antico ardor.
Is inextinguishable the-old ardor.
(Our former ardor is inextinguishable.)

Il fervido desiderio
The fervid desire

Quando verrà quel dì
When will-come that day
(When will the day come)

Che riveder potrò
That to-see-again I-will-be-able-to
(when I will be able to see you again)

Quel che l'amante cor tanto desia?
That which the-loving heart so-much desires?
(That which my loving heart desires so much?)

Che in sen t'accoglierò,
That in breast you-I-will-receive,
(That I will receive you in my breast,)

Ah, Bella fiamma d'amor, anima mia?
Ah, Beautiful flame of-love, soul my?
(Ah, Beautiful flame of love, my soul?)

Bellini
L'abbandono
The-abandonment

Solitario zeffiretto, A che movi i tuoi sospiri?
Solitary little-breeze, To whom you-move the your sighs?
(Solitary little breeze, to whom do your sighs move?)

a che?
to whom?
(to whom?)

Il sospiro a me sol lice, Chè, dolente ed infelice,
The sigh to me alone happy, How, painful and unhappy,
(The sigh, happy only to painful and unhappy me,)

Chiamo Dafne che non ode L'insoffribil mio martir.
I-call Daphne who not hears The-insufferable my martyrdom.
(I call Daphne who does not hear my insufferable martyrdom.)

Langue invan la mammoletta
Languish in-vain the little-violet
(The little violet,)

E la rosa e il gelsomino;
And the rose and the jasmine;
(rose and jasmine languish in vain;)

Lunge son da lui che adoro,
Far-away I-am from him whom I-adore,
(I am far away from him whom I adore,)

Non conosco alcun ristoro
Not I-understand any solace
(I do not have any solace)

Se non viene a consolarmi col bel guardo cilestrino.
If not he-comes to console-me with-the beautiful glance blue.
(If he does not come to console me with his beautiful blue eyes.)

Ape industre, che vagando
Bee industrious, that rambling
(Industrious bee, who always rambles)

Sempre vai di fior in fiore, Ascolta.
Always you-go from flower to flower, Listen.
(from flower to flower, Listen.)

Se lo scorgi ov'ei dimora,
If him you-find-out where-he lives,
(If you find out where he lives,)

Di' che rieda a chi l'adora.
Say that he-returns to who him-adores.
(tell him to return to the one who adores him.)

Bellini
L'Allegro Marinaro
The-Cheerful Sailor

Allor che azzurro il mar Sereno specchia il ciel, sereno,
When so blue the sea Serene mirrors the sky, serene,
(When the serene blue sea mirrors the sky, serene,)

Al tuo navil fedel Ritorna, o marinar, ritorna.
To-the your navy faithful Return, oh sailor, return.
(Return to your faithful navy, oh sailor, return.)

Tentiamo del piacer
Let-us-try of-the pleasure
(In pleasure, let us test)

Su l'onde la canzon, su l'onde,
On the-waves the song, on the-waves,
(the song of the waves, of the waves,)

Sfidiamo il flutto e il tuon
Let-us-challenge the wave and the thunder
(Happy adventurer, let us challenge)

Contenti avventurier, contenti.
Happy adventurer, happy.
(the wave and the thunder.)

Spera, spera, o marinar; La speranza è il nostro ben.
Hope, hope, o sailor, The hope is the our well-being.
(Hope, hope, o sailor, hope is our well-being.)

Ognun speri di tornar
Everyone hopes of returning
(Everyone hopes of returning)

De' suoi fidi ancora al sen.
Of their faithful-ones again to-the breast.
(to the breast of their faithful ones.)

Cinge il futuro un manto:
Enclose the future a cloak:
(Enclose the future in your cloak:)

Sol Dio saper potrà
Only God to-know will-be-able-to
(Only God will be able to know)

Chi fia che rivedrà L'antica madre in pianto.
Who is who will-see-again The-old mother in tears.
(Who again will see his old mother in tears.)

Allor che in ciel vedrem il nembo imperversar, Il nembo,
Then that in heaven we-will-see the cloud raging, The cloud,
(Then in heaven we will see the raging cloud, the cloud,)

Convien coraggio oprar: da forti griderem:
Convenient courage to-operate: with force we-will-cry:
(Gather courage to continue: forcefully we will cry:)

corraggio.
courage.
(courage.)

Oggi concenti e suon La sorte ci serbò, concenti;
Today melodies and sound The fate us kept, melodies;
(Today fate kept our melodies and sound, melodies;)

Doman mandar ci può Forse procelle e tuon, procelle.
Tomorrow to-send us can Perhaps storms and thunder, storms.
(Perhaps tomorrow it can send us storms and thunder, storms.)

Ma tornar vedrem sul mar, Pien di gioia, ancor quel sol
But to-return we-will on-the sea, Full of joy, still that sun
(But we will return to the sea, full of joy, still to that sun)

Che alla pace ridonar Ci dovrà del patrio suol.
Which to-the peace give-again Us will-give of-the native soil.
(Which again gives us peace on our native soil.)

Allor senza periglio La madre ascolterà
Then without peril The mother will-listen
(Now without fear the mother will listen to he)

Quella che a lei dirà
That-one who to her
(who will tell)

Storia de pianto il figlio.
Story of weeping the son.
(the story of the weeping son.)

La Farfalletta
The Little-Butterfly

Farfalletta, aspetta; Non volar con tanta fretta.
Little-Butterfly, wait; Not fly-away with so-much haste.
(Little butterfly, wait; don't fly away so quickly.)

Far del mal non ti vogl'io;
Make of-the harm not to-you wish-I;
(I don't want to harm you;)

Ferma, appaga il desir mio.
Stop, satisfy the desire my.
(Stop, satisfy my desire.)

Vo' baciarti e il cibo darti,
I-wish to-kiss-you and the food give-you,
(I want to kiss you, and give you food,)

Da' perigli preservarti.
From perils to-protect-you.
(protect you from perils.)

Di cristallo stanza avrai
From crystal room you-will-have
(You will have a crystal room)

E tranquilla ognor avrai.
And tranquillity always you-will-have.
(and always be tranquil.)

L'ali aurate, screzïate
The-wings resplendent, speckled
(I know April has given you)

So che Aprile t'ha ingemmate,
I-know that April you-has bejewelled,
(your resplendent speckled wings,)

Che sei vaga, vispa e snella,
Which are pretty, lively and thin,
(Which are pretty, lively and thin,)

Fra tue eguali la più bella.
Among your equals the most beautiful.
(Among butterflies the most beautiful.)

Ma crin d'oro ha il mio tesoro,
But hair of-gold has the my treasure,
(But my treasure has blond hair,)

Il fanciullo ch'amo, e adoro.
The boy whom-I-love, and I-adore.
(the boy whom I love and adore.)

E a te pari vispo e snello
And to you seem lively and thin
(And like you, lively and thin,)

Fra i suo' equali egli è il più bello.
Among the his equals he is the most beautiful.
(Among boys he is the most beautiful.)

Vo' capirti, ad esso offrirti;
I-wish to-understand-you, to him offer-you;
(I want to understand you, offer you to him;)

Più che rose, gigli, e mirti
More than roses, lilies, and myrtles
(More than roses, lilies, and myrtles)

Ti fia caro il mio fanciullo, Ed a lui sarai trastullo.
You are dear the my little-boy, And to him you-will-be toy.
(You are dear to my little boy, you will be a toy for him.)

Nell'aspetto e terso breast Roses,
In-the-look and terse breast Roses,
(My beloved has a little chest like roses,)

e gigli ha il mio diletto.
and lilies has the my beloved.
(and like lilies.)

Vieni, scampa da' perigli,
Come, escape from perils,
(Come, escape danger,)

Non cercar più rose e gigli.
Not search more roses and lilies.
(don't search any more among the roses and lilies.)

Bellini
La Ricordanza
The Remembrance

Era la notte, e presso di Colei
It-was the night, and near by With-her
(It was night, and with her nearby)

Che sola al cor mi giunse
That alone to-the heart me she-arrived
(That alone she came to my heart)

e vi sta sola,
and there she-stays alone.
(and there she stays alone.)

Con quel pianger che rompe la parola,
With that crying that breaks the word,
(With that crying that breaks the word,)

Io pregava mercede a martir miei.
I prayed reward to martyrdom my.
(I prayed for a reward for my martyrdom.)

Quand'Ella. chinando gli occhi bei,
When-She, bowing the eyes beautiful,
(When she, bowing her beautiful eyes,)

Disse, (e il membrarlo sol me, da me invola:)
Said, (and the remembrance-it only me, to me it-steals:)
(Said, (and my remembrance of it, it comes to me:))

Ponmi al cor la tua destra, e ti consola;
Put-me to-the heart the your right-hand, and you it-consoles;
(Put your right hand to my heart, and console yourself;)

Ch'io amo e te sol' amo intender dei.
That-I love and you alone I-love to-understand you-must.
(You must understand that I love you and you alone,)

Poi fatta, per amor, tremante e bianca,
Then done, for love, trembling and white,
(Then done, for love, trembling and white,)

In atto soavissimo mi pose
In attitude very-sweet me puts
(puts me in a very sweet mood)

La bella faccia sulla spalla mance.
The beautiful face on-the shoulder it-lacks.
(My shoulder lacks her beautiful.)

Se dopo il dolce assai più duol l'amero;
If after the sweetness enough more sorrow the-bitterness;
(If after enough sweetness the bitterness is more sorrowful;)

Se per me nullo istante a quel ripose,
If for me no instant to that repose,
(if for me no instant of that repose,)

Ah! quant'era in quell'ora il morir caro!
Ah! how-was in that-hour the death dear!
(Ah! how dear was death in that hour!)

Bellini
Malinconia, Ninfa gentile
Melancholy, Nymph gentle

Malinconia, Ninfa gentile,
Melancholy, Nymph gentle,
(Melancholy gentle Nymph,)

La vita mia consacro a te;
The life my I-consecrate to you;
(my life I consecrate to you;)

I tuoi piaceri chi tiene a vile,
The your pleasures which hold to worthless,
(Your pleasures which hold on to evil,)

Ai piacer veri nato non è.
To-the pleasures real born not is.
(are not born of real pleasures.)

Fonti e colline chiesi agli Dei;
Fountains and hills I-asked to-the Gods;
(Of these fountains and hills I asked the Gods;)

M'udirò alfine, pago io vivrò,
Myself-I-will-hear at-last, satisfied I will-live.
(I will hear myself at last, I will live satisfied.)

Nè mai quel fonte co' desir miei,
Neither never that fountain like desire my,
(Neither will be my desires like that fountain,)

Nè mai quel monte trapasserò,
Nor never that mountain I-will-traverse,
(nor ever will I traverse that mountain of melancholy.)

no, no, mai.
no, no, never.
(no, no, never.)

Ma rendi pur contento
Ah make still content

Ma rendi pur contento Della mia bella il core
Ah make still content Of-the my beautiful the heart
(Ah make the heart of my beautiful one still content)

E ti perdono, amore, Se lieto il mio non è.
And you I-will-forgive, love, If pleased the my not is.
(And you I will forgive, love, If you don't make me happy.)

Gli affanni suoi pavento Più degli affanni miei,
The sighs your I-fear More of-the sighs my,
(Your sighs I fear more than my sighs,)

Perchè più vivo in lei, Di quel ch'io vivo in me.
Because more I-live in you, Of more that-I-live in myself.
(Because I live more in you, than in myself.)

Per pietà, bell'idol mio
For pity, beautiful-idol my

Per pietà, bell'idol mio,
For pity, beautiful-idol my,
(Have pity, my beautiful idol,)

Non mi dir ch'io sono ingrato;
Not to-me say that-I am ungrateful;
(do not say that I am ungrateful;)

Infelice e sventurato Abbastanza il Ciel mi fa.
Unhappy and unlucky Enough the Heaven me makes.
(Heaven makes me unhappy and unlucky enough.)

Se fedele a te son io,
If faithful to you am I,
(If I am faithful to you,)

Se mi struggo ai tuoi bei lumi,
If myself I-consume to-the your beautiful eyes,
(If I consume myself with your beautiful eyes,)

Sallo amor, lo sanno i Numi,
Knows-it love, it they-know the Gods,
(You know it, love, the Gods know it,)

Il mio core, il tuo lo sa.
The my heart, the your it knows.
(my heart knows it, your heart knows it.)

Quando incise su quel marmo
When engraved on that marble

Questa è la valle, il sasso è questo in cui di Gilda
This is the valley, the tombstone is this in which of Gilda
(This is the valley where the name of Gilda, my wife,)

al nome unito Il mio nome è scolpito,
to-the name united The my name is carved,
(has been carved on the tombstone;)

e in queste guise,
and in these guises
(why in this guise did she)

Se tradirmi volea, perchè l'incise?
If to-betray-me she-wanted-to, why she-engrave-it?
(engrave it if she wanted to betray me?)

Quando incise su quel marmo L'infedele il nome mio,
When engraved on that marble The-unfaithful the name my,
(When my unfaithful name was engraved on that marble)

Invocando il cieco Dio, Fede eterna a me giurò.
Invoking the blind God, Faith eternal to me I-promised.
(Invoking the blind God, Eternal Faith I promised to myself.)

Spergiura! Sperguira!
Perjurer! Purjurer!
(Perjurer! Purjurer!)

e questa pietra Il mio nome addita ancora, spergiura!
and this stone The my name shows still, purjurer!
(and this stone still shows my name, purjurer!)

Ma l'idea di chi t'adora
But the-idea of whom you-she-adores
(But the idea of she)

Quando incise su quel marmo
                        (cont.)

Nel tuo sen si cancellò,
In-the your breast it cancelled,
(whom your breast adores is gone,)

Ahi, spergiura!
Alas, purjurer!
(Alas, purjurer!)

Sogno d'Infanzia
Dream of-Infancy

Soave sogno de' miei primi anni,
Sweet dream of my first years,
(Sweet dream of my first years,)

Di tue memorie, m'inebbria il cor;
Of your memories, me-elated the heart;
(With your memories my heart is elated;)

Solo in te spero nel mio dolor.
Only in you I-hope in-the my sorrow.
(Only in you have I hope in my sorrow.)

Nulla bandirti può dalla mente, Ignoto oggetto de' miei desiri;
Nothing forget-you can of-the mind, Unknown object of my
desires;
(Nothing can get you out of my mind, unknown desired
object;)

Qual m'eri allora, t'ho ancor presente Col tuo sorriso,
What to-me-were then, you-I-have still present With-the your
smile,
(I still have with my smile, what I had with you then,)

col tuo languor.
with-the your languor.
(with your lanquor.)

Sì, sempre, o cara, voglio adorarti,
Yes, always, oh dear-one, I-want to-adore-you,
(Yes, oh dear-one, I always want to adore you,)

E a tuoi bei squardi sempre pensar,
And of your beautiful glances always to-think,
(And always think of your beautiful glances,)

E a te miei giorni tutti sacrar.
And to you my days all to-dedicate.
(And to dedicate all my days to you.)

Sogno d'Infanzia
(cont.)

Quando dal cielo scesa io mirai
When from-the heavens descend I gazed-at
(I gazed at your beautiful and chaste figure)

La tua persona bella e pudica,
The your figure beautiful and chaste.
(when you descended from the heavens,)

Giovine allora, ah, non pensai
Young still, ah, not you-did-think
(Still young, ah, you did not think)

Che tardi un giorno fora l'amar.
That late one day I-would you-love.
(that one day I would love you.)

Rapido lampo tua debil vita Seco travolse dove si muor,
Rapid lightning your weak life With-you carry-away where
one dies,
(Rapid lightning carried your weak life away to death,)

Ed io ti chiamo, ti chiamo ancor.
And I to-you call, to-you I-call again.
(And I call to you, I call to you again.)

Pera l'istante quand'io ti vidi
From the-instant when-I you saw
(From the moment I saw you)

Pura qual giglio sulle prim'ore:
Pure as lily in-the first-hours:
(pure as a lily in its first hours:)

Tu ti slanciasti verso i tuoi lidi,
You you rushed-yourself toward the your shores,
(You rushed yourslf toward the shores,)

E di te, privo muore il mio cuor.
And of you, I-am-deprived dies the my heart.
(and, being deprived of you, my heart dies.)

Torna, Vezzosa Fillide
Return, Charming Fillide

Torna, vezzosa Fillide, Al caro tuo pastore;
Return, charming Fillide, To-the dear your shepherd;
(Come back, charming Fillide, to your dear shepherd;)

Lungi da tue pupille Pace non trova il cor,
Far from your eyes Peace not it-finds the heart,
(So far away from your eyes, my heart finds no peace,)

Al caro tuo soggiorno Io sempre volgo il piè'
To-the dear your journey I always turn the foot
(I always turn toward the direction of your dear journey)

E grido notte e giorno: Fillide mia dov'è? Fille mia?
And cry night and day: Fillide my where-is? Fille my?
(And day and night I cry: where is my Fillide? My Fille?)

Domando a quella sponda: Fillide mia che fa?
I-ask to that shore: Fillide my what you-do?
(I ask that shore: what are you doing, my Fillide?)

E par che mi risponda: Piange lontan da te!
And seems that to-me it-responds: She-cries far from you!
(And it seems to respond: far from you she cries!)

Domando a quello rio: Fillide mia Dov'è?
I-ask to that brook: Fillide my Where-is?
(I ask that brook: where is my Fillide?)

Con rauco mormorio Dice: piangendo sta.
With hoarse murmur it-Says: crying she-is.
(With hoarse murmur it says: she is crying.)

Il caro tuo sembiante, Fonte d'ogni piacere,
The dear your appearance, Fountain of-every pleasure,
(Your dear appearance, Fountain of every pleasure,)

Il miro ad ogni istante Impresso nel pensier;
It I-see at every instant impressed in-the thought;
(I see it at every moment impressed in my thoughts;)

Ma rimirando allora Ch'egli non è con me,
But looking-back then That-it not is with me,
(But then seeing that it is not with me,)

Grido piangendo ognora: Fillide mia dov'è?
I-yell crying always: Fillide my where-is?
(I always yell crying: where is my Fillide?)

Son fatte le mie pene Un tempestoso mare;
Are made the my pains A tempestuous sea:
(My pains make a tempestuous sea;)

Non trovo, amato bene,
Not I-find, beloved dear,
(Beloved dear,)

Chi le potrà calmar, nol trovo.
Who them can to-calm, not-it I-find.
(I can not find anyone to calm them.)

Che fa la morte, oh Dio, Che non mi chiama a sè?
What it-does the death, oh God, That not me it-calls to it?
(Oh God, why does death not call me?)

Gridar più non poss'io: Fillide mia Dov'è?
To-yell more not can-I: Fillide my Where-is?
(I cannot yell any more: where is my Fillide?)

Vaga luna, che inargenti
Pretty moon, who makes-silvery

Vaga luna, che inargenti
Pretty moon, who makes-silvery
(Pretty moon,)

Queste rive e questi fiori
These shores and these flowers
(who makes these shores and flowers silvery)

Ed inspiri agli elementi Il linguaggio dell'amor;
And inspires to-the elements The language of-the-love;
(And inspires the language of love to the elements;)

Testimonio or sei tu sola Del mio fervido desir,
I-tell now are you only Of-the my fervid desire,
(Of my fervid desire, now I tell only you,)

Ed a lei che m'innamora
And to you that I-am-falling-in-love
(And to you that I am falling in love)

Conta i palpiti e i sospir.
Count the palpitations and the sighs.
(Count the heart beats and the sighs.)

Dille pur che lontananza Il mio duol non può lenir,
Tell-her then that distance The my sorrow not can to-assuage,
(Then tell her that distance cannot assuage my sorrow,)

Che se nutro una speranza, Ella è sol, sì,
That if I-feed a hope, She is only, yes,
(That I feed upon a hope, she is the only one, yes,)

Ella è sol nell'avvenir.
She is only in-the-future.
(she is the only one in my future.)

Dille pur che giorno e sera
Tell-her also that day and evening
(Also tell her that day and night)

Conto l'ore del dolor,
I-count the-hours of-the grief,
(I count the hours of grief,)

Che una speme lusinghiera Mi conforta nell'amor.
That a hope enticing Me comforts in-the-love.
(That the enticing hope of her love comforts me.)

Vanne, o rosa fortunata
Go, oh rose fortunate

Vanne, o rosa fortunata, A posar di Nice in petto
Go, oh rose fortunate, To rest in Nice in breast
(Go, oh fortunate rose, to rest in the heart of Nice)

Ed ognun sarà costretto La tua sorte invidïar.
And everyone will-be compelled The your fate to-envy.
(And everyone will be compelled to envy your fate.)

Oh, se in te potessi anch'io Trasformarmi un sol momento;
Oh, if in you could also-I Transform-me a sole moment;
(Oh, if you could also transform me in a single moment;)

Non avrai più bel contento Questo core a sospirar,
Not will-have more beautiful content This heart to sigh,
(My heart would not sigh from a more beautiful fullness,)

Ma tu inchini dispettosa, Bella rosa impallidita,
But you bow scornful, Beautiful rose fading,
(But you scornfully bow, Beautiful fading rose,)

La tua fronte scolorita Dallo sdegno e dal dolor.
The your face colorless From-the anger and from-the sorrow.
(Your face colorless from anger and sorrow.)

Bella rosa, è destinata Ad entrambi un'ugual sorte:
Beautiful rose, is destined To both an-equal fate:
(Beautiful rose, we are both destined to an equal fate:)

Là trovar dobbiam la morte, Tu d'invidia ed io d'amor.
There to-find we-must the death, You of-envy and I of-love.
(There we must find death, you of envy and I of love.)

Donaudy
Ah, che odor di buono...
Ah, what smell of goodness...

Ah, che odor di buono quando voi passate,
Ah, what smell of goodness when you pass,
(Ah, what a smell of goodness as you pass,)

doviziosa più che una fiorente estate!
rich more that a flourishing summer!
(richer than a flourishing summer!)

Voi credete allora che uno sguardo basti
You believe then that a glance stops
(Do you believe that a glance will)

per chi s'innamora a calmar sue brame?
for who himself-is-in-love to calm his desires?
(calm the desires of one who is in love?)

Ed invece con che fame alle spalle io vi cammino!
And instead with what hunger to-the shoulders I to-you walk!
(And instead I walk to you with such hunger in my body!)

Ma, più vengo a voi vicino, più il mio stomaco s'allunga...
But, more I-come to you close, more the my stomach it-
extends...
(But the closer I come to you, the more my stomach drops...)

Se sapeste come punga il desio che voi destate,
If you-had-known how sharp the desire that you stirred,
(If you knew how strongly you stirred my desire,)

certo avreste più pietate!
certainly you-might-have more pity!
(you might certainly have more pity!)

Madonnetta, perdonate l'importuno; ma, per adorarvi,
Little-woman, pardon the-trouble; but, to adore-you,
(Young lady, excuse me; but, by loving you,)

sto così a digiuno!
I-am like-this to fasting!
(I am fasting myself!)

Ah, mai non cessate...
Ah, never not stop...

Ah, mai non cessate dal vostro parlar,
Ah, never not stop from-the your talking,
(Ah, do not stop talking,)

o labbra desiate ond'io folle vo':
oh lips desired by-which-I mad want;
(oh desired lips which I madly want;)

coi miei delle vostre parole vo' far
with-the my of-the your words I-wish to-make
(with your words I want to make)

un dolce guanciale su cui dormirò.
a sweet pillow on which I-will-sleep.
(a sweet pillow on which I will sleep.)

O sonni beati da niun mai sognati
Oh dreams blessed of no-one ever dreamed
(Oh blessed dreams that no one ever dreamed)

che su quel guanciale dormendo farò,
that on that pillow sleeping I-will-make,
(that on that pillow I will fall asleep,)

vicino al tuo cor, il dolce,
close to-the your heart, the sweet,
(close to your heart, the sweetness,)

desiato mio sogno d'amor. Ah!
desired my dream of-love. Ah!
(I will have my desired dream of love. Ah!)

Donaudy
Amor mi fa cantare...
Love me makes to-sing...

Amor mi fa cantare per dir le laudi ascose
Love me makes to-sing to tell the praises hidden
(Love makes me sing, telling the hidden praises)

di due pupille chiare e di due labbra oziose.
of two eyes bright and of two lips idle.
(of two bright eyes and of two idle lips.)

S'io penso a quello sguardo, il sol mi sembra offenso;
If-I think of that image, the sun to-me seems offensive;
(If I think of that image, the sun seems offensive to me;)

e tutto avvampo ed ardo se a quelle labbra penso.
and all ablaze and ardent if to those lips I-think.
(and if I think of those lips, I am all ablaze and ardent.)

Se poi, siccome suole, mi guarda e parla un po',
If then, as grounds, to-me he/she-looks and he/she-speaks a little,
(If then, to the ground he/she looks and speaks a little,)

son come cera al sole: tutto mi liquefo.
I-am like wax to-the sun: all me melts.
(I am like wax in the sunlight: all of me melts.)

Ma invan le trotto dietro da quasi un anno intero;
But in vain the journey backwards to like a year entire;
(But in vain the journey back like an entire year ago;)

invan, cambiando metro, mi mostro audace o altero.
in-vain, exchanging meter, me I-show audacious or proud.
(in vain, changing pace, I am audacious or proud.)

Se le rivolgo un motto, dal rider non si regge...
If it I-turn a word, of-the laughing not to endure...
(If I make a joke, I cannot endure the laughter...)

Le scrivo uno strambotto?   Lo legge e non lo legge.
It I-write a folk-song?   It reads and not it reads.
(If I write a folk song?   It sounds good, and it doesn't.)

Amor mi tiene in pugno...
Love to-me holds in fist...

Amor mi tiene in pugno, mi gira, rigira,
Love me holds in fist, me it-turns, it-re-turns,
(Love's fist holds me, turns me, turns me again,)

m'annusa e poi sospira...Ahimè, che brutto segno!
me-it-discovers and then it-sighs...Alas, that brutal sign!
(and then discovers me and sighs...Alas, that brutal sign!)

Son già forse indegno d'entrar nel suo regno
I-am already perhaps unworthy to-enter in-the your reign
(Perhaps I am already unworthy to enter into your reign)

e starvi ancora a gironzar?
and you-stay still to lounge?
(and you still stay to lounge?)

Eppur se adesso son sì dimesso, sparuto,
And-yet if now I-am so neglected, thin,
(And yet if I am now so neglected, thin,)

gibbuto, sol buono a lagrimar, gli è per quei sospiri
humped, only good to cry, the is for those sighs
(misshapen, only good to cry, it is for those sighs)

e i lunghi martiri cui
and the long torments of-them
(and their long torments)

senza ricetto amor m'ha costretto...
without retreat love me-has forced...
(without retreat that love has forced me...)

Ma per un po' ch'io tento qual fui di ritornar...,
But for a little that-I try that I-was of returning...,
(But for a little I was trying to return...,)

vedrete a cento le donzellette
you-will-see to hundred the little-shepherdesses
(you will see a hundred little shepherdesses)

attorno a me cascar!
turning to-me falling!
(turning around me falling!)

D'amor ta l'è il costume davvero
Of-love so-much it-is the custom in-truth
(It is so much the custom in the terrible truth)

tremendo che vivasi morendo
terrible that lives-it dying
(of love that it lives dying)

e che si mora vivi, di tutto già privi,
and that one dies you-live, of all already lacking,
(so that one dies, you live, already lacking all,)

persin quando ancora molto c'è da assaporar...
even when still much it-is to enjoy...
(even when still it is much to enjoy...)

Per cui se adesso son sì dimesso, paruto,...
For them if now I-am so neglected, thin,...
(for them if I am now so neglected, thin,...)

Amorosi miei giorni...
Lovers my days...

Amorosi miei giorni,
Lovers my days,
(Lovers of my days,)

chi vi potrà mai più scordar,
who you will-be-able-to never more to-forget,
(who you will never more be able to forget you,)

or che di tutti i beni adorni,
now that of all the goods you-adorn,
(now that you adorn all goodness,)

date pace al mio core e profumo ai pensieri?
make peace to-the my heart and perfume to-the thoughts?
(and perfume my thoughts? make peace in my heart)

Poter così, finchè la vita avanza,
To-be-able-to thus, until the life advances,
(Thus to be able, until life ends,)

non temer più gli affanni
not fear more the pains
(to no more fear the pains)

d'una vita d'inganni, sol con questa speranza:
of-a life of-deceits, alone with this hope:
(of a life of deceits, alone with this hope:)

che un suo squardo sia tutto il mio splendor
that a your glance is all the my splendor
(that your glance is all my splendor)

e un suo sorriso sia tutto il mio tesoro!
and a your smile is all the my treasure!
(and your smile is all my treasure!)

Chi di me più beato,
Who of me more blessed,
(Who to me more blessed,)

se accanto a sè così non ha
if close-by to himself thus not he-has
(if close to him thus he has)

un dolce e caro oggetto amato, si che ancor non può dire
a sweet and dear object beloved, himself that still not can say
(a sweet and dear beloved object, himself still cannot say)

di saper cos'è amore?
to know what-is love?
(to know what love is?)

Certo un po' di cielo colse...
I-search a little of heaven with-him...

Certo un po' di cielo colse chi ti fe'
I-search a little of heaven with-him who to-you faithful
(I search a little of heaven with him whose beautiful eyes)

quegli occhi belli, ed al sole un raggio
those eyes beautiful, and to-the sun a ray
(are faithful to you, and took away the chance)

tolse per far biondi quei capelli.
took-away to make blond those hairs.
(for the sun's ray to make those hairs blond.)

Ma, compiuta l'opra esterna,
But, accomplished the-task external,
(But after the task was accomplished,)

fu poi preso da torpore e,
was then taken of numbness and,
(I was then taken by numbness and,)

per farti un po' di cuore, nulla agli angeli levò.
for to-make-you a little of heart, nothing to-the angels rose.
(to make you a little heart, nothing rose to the angels.)

Benedetto, ad ogni modo, chi al mondo ti donò!
Blessed, to-the every way, who to-the world you gave!
(Be blessed, in every way, he who gave you to the world!)

Ero ben felice e pago della sorte mia primiera.
I-was well happy and pleased of-the fate my first.
(I was very happy and pleased with my first fate,)

Pastorello, m'era svago
Shepherd, to-me-was amusement
(Shepherd, who amused me)

zufolar mattina e sera.
whistling morning and night.
(day and night by whistling.)

Ma, dal giorno che t'ho vista,
But, in-the day which you-I-have seen,
(But in the day in which I saw you,)

cambiò tutto per incanto;
I-changed all to enchantment;
(I changed all to enchantment:)

più non rido, più non canto:
more not I-laugh, more not I-sing;
(I no longer laugh, I no longer sing;)

sol compagno m'è il dolor!
only like to-me-is the sorrow!
(I am like sorrow only!)

Benedetto, ad ogni modo, quel tal giorno sia per me!
Blessed, to-the every way, that so-much day is to me!
(Be blessed, in every way, that day so full is mine!)

Come l'alladoletta...
Like the-little-lark...

Come l'allodoletta per li prati,
Like the-little-lark through the meadows,
(Like the little lark of the meadows,)

così fugge la pace e l'allegranza da un cor gentile
so it-flies the peace and the-contentment from a heart gentle
(so flies peace and contentment from a gentle heart)

in cui sol regna amore!
in which only reigns love!
(in which only love reigns!)

Passa ogni gioia, passa ogni dolore
It-passes every joy, it-passes every pain
(It surpasses every joy, it surpasses every pain)

da un cor gentile in cui sol regna amore;
from a heart gentle in which only reigns love;
(from a gentle heart in which only love reigns;)

e l'alma che ne sente la gravanza,
and the-soul that not feels the burden,
(and the soul that does not, feels the burden,)

sen' muore di gelo come un fior!
feels-it dies of cold like a flower!
(and feels like dying of cold like a flower!)

Donaudy
Cuor mio, cuor mio non vedi...
Heart my, heart my not you-see...

Cuor mio, cuor mio non vedi che, quando amor ti coglie,
Heart my, heart my not you-see that, when love to-you hits,
(My heart, my heart don't you see that when love hits you,)

non gioie son, ma tedii; non fremiti, ma doglie?
not joys I-have, but boredom; not tremble-you, but pains?
(I have no joys, but boredom; don't you tremble with pains?)

E smetti allora un poco di fare il cascamorto!
And you-give-up then a little of making the pursuit!
(So then give up for a little while making pursuits!)

Non ti sei dunque accorto che amar e un brutto gioco?
Not you know then shrewd that love is a brutal game?
(Then being shrewd don't you know that love is a brutal game?)

Ma qual vid'io donzella di pei più bella e pura?...
Ah that see-I shepherdess of to-the more beautiful and pure?...
(Ah do I see a shepherdess more beautiful and pure?...)

Ahimè, ho gran paura che ci ricaschero!
Alas, I-have great fear that they will-re-fall-in-love!
(Alas, I have great fear that they will fall in love again!)

Par che non riesca vano
By that not it-rebaits vain
(So that it does not in vain rebait,)

fuggir l'amato incanto...
to-flee the-lover enchanted...
(flee from the enchanted lover...)

Ma come andar lontano e non restarle accanto?
But like going far-away and not being-you nearby?
(Ah, like going far away and not being nearby you?)

No, no; è miglior consiglio, l'amor vedendo a zonzo,
No, no; is better advice, the-love wandering to about,
(No, no; it is better advice, love wandering about,)

fuggir come un coniglio o fargli un cuor di bronzo.
to-flee like a coward or make-them a heart of bronze.
(to flee like a coward or make them a heart of bronze.)

Donaudy
Date abbiente al mio dolore...
Give light to-the my pain...

Date abbiente al mio dolore, care luci disdegnose,
Give light to-the my pain, dear eyes disdainful,
(Give light to my pain, dear disdainful eyes,)

poi che un vostro sguardo pose dolci pene nel mio cuore.
then that a your glance put sweet pains in-the my heart.
(then put sweet pains in my heart with your glance.)

Per le pene dell'amore voi sapete, luci care,
For the pains of-the-love you know, eyes dear,
(For you know the pains of love, dear eyes,)

ciò che val d'essere
that which is-worth of-being
(that is worthy)

avere d'un sol sguardo adulatore.
to-have of-a single look flattering.
(of having a single flattering glance.)

Dormendo stai...
Sleeping you-remain...

Dormendo stai con le braccia inarcate,
Sleeping you-remain with the arms closed,
(You stay sleeping with your arms closed,)

quasi una rosa in desio di sbocciar;
like a rose in desire of blossom;
(like a rose desiring to bloom;)

e non ascolti le liete brigate che van cantando
and not you-hear the joyful brigands who go singing
(and don't hear the joyful brigands who go about singing)

le lor maggiolate.
the their dirty-songs-of-May.
(their dirty song of May.)

Niuna parola ti dice questo sospirar
No-one word to-you says this breathing
(To my violet, no one breathes a word)

di mia viola? Tempo è venuto di goder maggio!
of my violet? Time is come to enjoy May!
(of this? The time has come to enjoy May!)

Questo è il messaggio d'ogni liuto...
This is the message of-every lute...
(This is the message of every lute...)

Ah! Odi il mio canto?
Ah! You-hear the my song?
(Ah! Do you hear my song?)

Che fai dunque lì ancor ascosa?
That makes then there still secret?
(That there then is still a secret?)

Fresca e odorosa, t'aspetta amor!
Fresh and fragrant, you-it-awaits love!
(Fresh and fragrant, love awaits you!)

Dormendo stai...
(cont.)

Se vieni meco per esta contrada,
If you-come with-me to pass country,
(If you come with me to traverse the country,)

diran che accanto sbocciato m'è un fior e ch'io l'adduco
say that nearby bloomed to-me-is a flower and that-I it-bring
(say that nearby a flower bloomed to me and that I bring it)

così per istrada a bere un sorso di fresca rugiada,
thus to initiate to drink a sip of fresh dew,
(thus to initiate drinking a sip of fresh dew,)

mentre i garzoni ci seguiranno sospirando lor canzoni.
while the youths they follow sighing their songs.
(while the youths follow sighing their songs.)

E Fille m'ha detto...
And Filli to-me-has told...

E Filli m'ha detto: levatevi, amanti;
And Filli me-has told: get-up-you, lovers;
(And Filli has told me: get up, lovers:)

son tolti gl'incanti, non regna più Amor!
are removed the-enchantments, not reigns more Eros!
(enchantments are gone, Eros reigns no longer!)

Ma Filli al mio petto stringevo anelante,
But Filli to-the my breast I-used-to-squeeze gasping,
(But Filli used to gaspingly squeeze to my breast,)

e tutta tremante m'ha detto essa allor:
and all quivering me-has told she then:
(and, all quivering, she then has told me:)

"Amore è un arciero che mai perde li sproni od il cimiero!"
"Love is an archer who never loses the spurs or the helmet!"
("Love is an archer who never loses his spurs or his helmet!")

Donaudy
Freschi luoghi, prati aulenti...
Cool places, meadows perfumed...

Freschi luoghi, prati aulenti, rimanete sempre in fior;
Cool places, meadows perfumed, remaining always in flower;
(Cool places, perfumed meadows, always staying in flower;)

che l'estate non vi sementi,
which the-summer not you sow,
(which summer does not sow,)

che l'autunno non vi travolga,
which the-autumn not you overturns,
(which autumn does not change,)

che la morta stagion
that the death season
(I hope that winter)

non tolga tanto magico splendor.
not it-takes-away so-much magic splendor.
(doesn't take away so much magic spendor.)

Voglio un dì vagar
I-wish one day to-wander
(One day I wish to wander)

con lei fra sì verde soavità,
with her among such green softness,
(with her among such green softness,)

quando alfin gli affani miei lei d'intender mostrerà.
when at-last the pangs my she to-intend will-show.
(when at last I will show my desires intended for her.)

Freschi luoghi, prati aulenti, rimanete sempre in fior;
Cool places, meadows perfumed, remaining always in flower;
(Cool places, perfumed meadows, always staying in flower;)

che nessuna stagion vi tolga tanto magico splendor.
that no-one season you takes-away so-much magic splendor.
(I hope that no season takes away so much splendor from
you.)

E voi pur, ruscelli chiari, che di già correte al mar,
And you also, brooks clear, which of already runs to-the sea,
(And you also, clear brooks, which already run to the sea,)

di vostra acque non siate avari
of your water you not will-be miserly
(will not be miserly with your water)

nelle tarde stagion dell'anno,
in-the late season of-the-year,
(in the late season of the year,)

non unite anche voi l'inganno d'un sì breve prosperar.
not unite also you the-deceit of-a so brief to-prosper.
(don't join the deceit of so brief a prosperity.)

Vo' specchiarmi un dì
I-want to-look-myself one day
(I want to see myself with her)

con lei nelle vostre chiarità,
with her in-the your brightness,
(one day in your brightness,)

quando alfin gli affanni miei lei d'intender mostrerà.
when at-last the pangs my she to-understand will-show.
(when at last she will understand my desires for her.)

Donaudy
Luoghi sereni e cari...
Places serene and dear...

Luoghi sereni e cari, io vi ritrovo quali ai bei
Places serene and dear, I you refind those to-the beautiful
(Dear and serece places, I find you again, beautiful lost)

dì lasciai di giovinezza! Gli stessi amati aspetti
days I-lost of youth! Those same lovers await
(days of youth! Those same lovers await)

ovunque il passo io muovo...Sol non mi punge ancor
everywhere the step I move...Sun not me stings still
(everywhere I make a step...The sun no longer stings me)

che l'amarezza dei mesti giorni in cui i tormenti
that the-grief of-the dejected days in which the torments
(with the grief of dejected days in which torments)

d'un triste inganno insegnato m'hanno pei primi cosa
of-a sad deceit taught me-they-have for-the first time
(of a sad deceit taught me for the first time)

al mondo è dolor! Lungi da voi fuggito allor
to-the world is sorrow! Far from you I-flew then
(that the world is sorrow! Then far from you I fled)

cercai di trovar pace al mio tradito core.
I-searched to find peace to-the my betrayed heart.
(I searched to find peace for my betrayed heart.)

Andai fin oltre mare, ed altre donne amai...
I-went far beyond sea, and other women loved...
(I went far beyond the sea, and loved other women...)

Ma nulla può lenire quel dolore ch'è piaga viva
But none could assuage those pains which-is scared lives
(But no one could assuage that pain which lives scared)

ogni core d'amante che nell'amore aveva ugual fede
every heart of-love which in-the-love had equal faith
(in every loving heart which in love had equal faith)

che pregando il Signor!
that prayed the Lord!
(that prayed to the Lord!)

Madonna Renzuola...
Madame Renzuola...

Madonna Renzuola, prendete l'orcetto, venite alla fonte,
Madame Renzuola, take the-jar, come to-the fountain,
(Madame Renzuola, take the jar, come to the fountain,)

chè grande è il diletto di stare aspettando
which large is the delight to stay awaiting
(which is a great delight to stay waiting for)

che l'acqua zampilli fra i villici idilli
that the-water gushing among the villagers idyllic
(the gushing water among the idyllic villagers)

che intrecciansi là.
which intertwine there.
(who mingle there.)

Chi sa non sentiate che pene ho nel cor,
Who knows not to-feel that pain I-have in-the heart,
(Who doens't know the felling of pain I have in my heart,)

vedendo e ascoltando parlare d'amor...
seeing and listening to-speak of-love...
(seeing and listening to talk of love...)

Niun'altra speranza più viver mi fa!
No-one-other hope more to-live me makes!
(No other hope makes me live!)

Lasciate lo specchio, venite in guarnello,
Leave the mirror, come in petticoats,
(Leave the mirror, come in petticoats,)

le treccie disciolte, senz'ombra d'orpello:
the tresses free, without-shadow of-ribbon:
(the tresses free, without shadow of ribbon:)

vedrete a quant'altre delizie
you-will-see to how-many-other delights
(you will see how many other delights)

c'invita la semplice vita
they-invite the simple life
(invite the simple life)

dei campi e...chi sa?
of-the fields and...who knows?
(in the fields and...who knows?)

che sì affranto mi tiene, persin quella mi lascia,
that so broken me holds, even that to-me leaves,
(that holds me so broken, that even leaves me,)

onde almen nutrivo il core, pietosa speranza
by-which at-least I-feed the heart, pitious hope
(by which at least I feed my heart, pitious hope)

che anche al misero avanza
that also to-the misery increases
(that also misery increases)

perchè gli sia men crudo il dolor!
because it is less cruel the sorrow!
(because it is less cruel than sorrow!)

O del mio amato ben...
Oh of-the my loved well...

O del mio amato ben perduto incanto!
Oh of-the my loved well lost enchantment!
(Oh lost enchantment of my dear beloved!)

Lungi è dagli occhi miei chi m'era gloria e vanto!
Far is from-the eyes my who to-me-was glory and pride!
(He who was my glory and pride is far from my eyes!)

Or per le mute stanze sempre la/lo cerco
Now through the mute rooms always her/him I-search
(Now I always search for her/him through quiet rooms)

e chiamo con pieno il cor di speranze...
and I-call with full the heart of hopes...
(and I call out with my heart full of hopes...)

Ma cerco invan, chiamo invan!
But I-search in-vain, I-call in-vain!
(But I search in vain, I call in vain!)

E il pianger m'è sì caro,
And the weeping to-me-is so dear,
(And weeping is so dear to me,)

che di pianto sol nutro il cor.
that of tears alone I-feed the heart.
(that on tears alone I feed my heart.)

Mi sembra, senza lei/lui, triste ogni loco.
To-me it-seems, without her/him, sad every place.
(Without her/him, every place seems sad to me.)

Notte mi sembra il giorno; mi sembra gelo il foco.
Night to-me seems the day; to-me seems cold the fire.
(Night seems like the day to me; the fire seems cold to me.)

Se pur talvolta spero di darmi ad altra cura,
If yet sometimes I-hope to give-me an other cure,
(If sometimes I hope to give myself another cure,)

sol mi tormenta un pensiero:
only me it-torments one thought:
(only one thought torments me:)

ma senza lei/lui, che farò?
but without her/him, what will-I-do?
(but without her/him, what will I do?)

Mi par così la vita
To-me it-seems thus the life
(To me it seems that life like)

vana cosa senza il mio ben.
vain thing without the my beloved.
(this is a vain thing without my beloved.)

Ognun ripicchia e nicchia...
Everyone insists and hesitates...

Ognun ripicchia e nicchia ognor
Everyone insists and hesitates always
(Everyone insists and always hesitates)

su un caso strano a dir.
on a story strange to tell.
(on a strange story to tell.)

Ma perchè, ma cos'è, che tanto amor dovea così finir?
But why, but what-is, that so-much love had so to-end?
(But why, but what is it, that so much love had to end thus?)

Or io voglio la mia storia raccontar tanto buffa ell'è:
Now I want the my story to tell so funny it-is:
(Now I want to tell my story which is so funny:)

Me ne givo un dì con Monna Lapa, insiem,
Me with-her I-went one day with Monna Lapa, together,
(One day I went with Monna Lapa, together,)

che sì cara m'era al cor,
who so dear to-me-she-was to-the heart,
(who was very dear to my heart,)

per i campi a racoglier fior...
through the fields to gather flowers...
(through the fields to gather flowers...)

Ma la storia comincia qui.
But the story starts here.
(But the story starts here.)

U'! cos'è quel ch'io veggo là? Un grillo o un rusignuol?
Ah! what-is that that-I see there? A cricket or a nightingale?
(Ah! what is that that I see there? A cricket or a nightingale?)

Più bel ve', più bel ve'!
More beautiful I-see, more beautiful I-see!
(A more beautiful one I see, I see a more beautiful one!)

La mia beltà sedette su un poggiuol.
The my beauty sat on a hill.
(My beauty sat on a hill.)

Lei sperava di poter così goder il divin cantor,
She hoped of being-able thus to-enjoy the divine singer,
(She hoped that this way she would be able to enjoy the divine singer,)

ma al trillar del grillo
but to-the trilling of-the cricket
(but with the trilling of the cricket)

e al pronto suo balzar diede un grido,
and to-the quick his leaping she-gave a scream,
(and his quick leaping, she screamed,)

e nel fuggir,
and in-the fleeing,
(and in fleeing,)

sù ove prima seggea cascò...
on where before she-was-sitting I-fell...
(on the same place where before she was sitting, I fell...)

E la storia finisce lì.
And the story ends there.
(And the story ends there.)

Or che le rèdole...
Now that the walkways...

Or che le rèdole verdi ritornano,
Now that the walkways green return,
(Now that the green walkways return,)

che veston fiori i cespi ancor,
that clothe flowers the bushes also,
(that clothe the flowers and also the bushes,)

d'intrecciar danze tempo è tornato;
of-intertwining dances time is returned;
(the time for intertining dances has returned;)

vieni sul prato, fiore tra i fior.
come on-the meadow, flowers among the flowers.
(come to the meadow, it flowers among the flowers.)

Giga o furlana vieni a danzare, di tarlatana tutta vestita.
Jig or furlana come to dance, of cotton-clothes all dressed.
(Come dance the jig or the furlana, all dressed in cotton
clothes.)

Stringerti per la vita parlandoti d'amore:
Come-close-you for the life speaks-to-you of-love:
(Come close for life speaks to you of love:)

altro dolzore non so sperar.
other sweetness not I-know to-hope.
(of other sweetness I do not know how to hope.)

Nel lieve fremito d'un giro destasi tale un diletto,
In-the soft trembling of-a turn awakes such a delight,
(In the soft trembling of a turn such delight awakes,)

un tale ardor, ch'ogni altro affanno è presto obliato;
a such ardor, that-every other pain is immediately forgotten;
(such ardor, that every other pain is immediately forgotten;)

vieni sul prato, fiore tra i fior.
come on-the meadow, flowers among the flowers.
(come to the meadow, it flowers among the flowers.)

Donaudy
Perchè dolce, caro bene
Why sweet, dear beloved

Perchè dolce, caro bene stizzosetta sei con me,
Why sweet, dear beloved irritable you-are with me,
(Why, sweet, dear beloved, are you irritable with me,)

dacchè sai le dure pene
since you-know the cruel pains
(since you know the cruel pains)

che nel cor soffr'io per te?
which in-the heart suffer-I for you?
(which in my heart I suffer for you?)

Mordemi! Baciami! Battimi! Abbraciami! Ah! Pietà!
Bite-me! Kiss-me! Hit-me! Embrace-me! Ah! Pity!
(Bite me! Kiss me! Hit me! Embrace me! Ah! Have pity!)

O ti prendi servitù, o mi rendi libertà!
Oh you take servitude, or to-me you-give liberty!
(Oh accept my servitude, or give me freedom!)

Se ti parlo non m'ascolti;
If to-you I-speak not me-you-listen;
(If I speak to you, you don't listen;)

se ti guardo, guardi in giù;
if to-you I-look, you-look in down;
(if I look at you, you look down;)

ma non guardo e allor ti volti;
but not I-look and then you turn;
(but when I don't look at you, you turn away;)

ma non parlo, e parti tu!
but not I-speak, and leave you!
(and when I don't speak to you, you leave!)

Perduta ho la speranza...
Lost I-have the hope...

Perduta ho la speranza in voi mirare,
Lost I-have the hope in you to-look,
(I have lost the hope of looking at you,)

e di speranza sola nutrivo il core!
and of hope alone I-used-to-feed the heart!
(and I used to feed my heart on hope alone!)

Ahimè! Ah! come farò se per amare,
Alas! Ah! how I-will-do if to love,
(Alas! Ah! how will I do if to love,)

la fede ho già smarrita, la fede nell'amore?
the faith I-have already lost, the faith in-the-love?
(I have already lost faith, faith in love?)

Donaudy
Quando'il tuo diavol nacque...
When-the your wretch born...

Quand'il tuo diavol nacque
When-the your wretch born
(When your wretch was born,)

il mio già andava a scuola,
the my already was-going to school,
(mine was already going to school,)

sicchè a un'astuzia sola il cor mai non soggiaque.
therefore to an-astuteness alone the heart never not enslaved.
(therefore only to astuteness was my heart ever enslaved.)

T'inghingheri, ti buzzichi,
You-dress-up, you stirred,
(You dress up, you budge,)

fai per piacermi e stuzzichi...
you-do to pleasure-me and you-tease...
(you pleasure me and you tease...)

Ma sai cos'è l'amor? Cos'è?
But you-know what-is the-love? What-is?
(But do you know what love is? What it is?)

E un certo non so che niun comanda al cor.
Is a certainty not I-know that no-one commands to-the heart.
(It is a certainty that I don't know how it commands my heart.)

Se finsi un solo istante d'assecondar tue mire,
If ends-it a sole instant to-favor your images,
(If it ends in a single instant to favor your images,)

fu per non far poltrire un cor d'antico amante.
was for not to-make lazy a heart of-former lover,
(it was not to make the heart of a former lover lazy,)

Nessuno mai s'attedia giuocando tal commedia.
No-one ever himself-wearies playing so-much comedy.
(No one ever wearies himself playing so much comedy.)

Quando ti rivedrò...
When of-you will-return...

Quando ti rivedrò,
When of-you will-return,
(When will you return,)

infida amante che mi fosti sì cara?
unfaithful lover who to-me was so dear?
(unfaithful lover who was so dear to me?)

Tante lagrime ho pianto or che altrui ci separa,
So-many tears I-have cried now that another us separates,
(Now that someone else separates us, I have cried so many
tears,)

che temo sia fuggita ogni gioia per sempre di mia vita.
that I-fear is flown every joy for always from my life.
(that I fear that every joy is gone from my life forever.)

Eppur più mi dispero, più ritorno a sperare.
Yet more to-me I-despair, more I-return to hoping,
(Yet the more I despair, the more I return to hoping,)

Più t'odio nel pensiero e più ancora
More you-I-hate in-the thought and more still
(The more I hate you in my thoughts, the more still)

l'anima mia torna ad amar.
the-soul my turns to love.
(my soul turns to love.)

Donaudy
Quelle labbra non son rose...
Those lip not are roses...

Quelle labbra, mia signora, non son rose maggioline;
Those lip, my lady, not are roses of-May;
(Those lips, my lady, are not roses of May;)

(vi dicevo sempre allora.)
(to-you I-said always then.)
((I always said to you.))

Ci son rose senza spine?
There are roses without thorns?
(Are there roses without thorns?)

Ma le ho baciate or ed ho pensato:
But them I-have kissed now and I-have thought:
(But now that I have kissed them, I have thought:)

non son di rose un paio, ma sono un gran rosaio!
not they-are of roses a pair, ah they-are a big rosebush!
(they are not a pair of roses, ah! they are a big rosebush!)

Sicchè persin ne ho insanguinato il cor, Ah!
Therefore even of-it I-have blood-stained the heart, Ah!
(So that with it I have blood stained my heart, Ah!)

Sento nel core...
I-feel in-the heart...

Sento nel core certo dolore
I-feel in-the heart certain pain
(I feel in my heart a certain pain)

che la mia pace turbando va.
that the my peace upsetting gets.
(that upsets my peace.)

Splende una face che l'alma accende
Shines a face that the-soul lights
(A face shines that lights my soul)

se non è amore, amor sarà.
if not is love, love it-will-be.
(if it isn't love, love it will be.)

Donaudy
Se tra l'erba...
If among the-grass...

Se tra l'erba un rio novello
If among the-grass a brook new
(If among the grass a new brook)

balza e corre verso il mare,
leaps and runs toward the sea,
(leaps and runs toward the sea,)

se rinverda il practicello, primavera è per tornare...
if regreens the small-meadow, spring is for returning...
(if the small meadow regreens, spring is returning...)

Coi tuoi riccioli vaganti scherza il mite zefiretto,
With-the your curls wandering it-plays the mild little-breeze,
(With your wandering curls the mild little breeze plays,)

mentre vai pei verzicanti prati
while you-go through-the turning-green meadows
(while you go through the billowing green meadows)

stretta sul mio petto;
pressed on-the my breast;
(pressed on my breast;)

bella m'è la vita allor!
beautiful to-me-is the life then!
(then life is beautiful to me!)

Ma se tutto discolora
But if everything discolors
(But if everything discolors)

e s'oscura l'orizzonte, piove a valle,
and it-darkens the-horizon, it-rains to heavily.
(and the horizon darkens, it rains heavily,)

tuona a monte; triste il verno torna ancora...
it-thunders to shaking; sad the winter returns again...
(it thunders shaking; sadly the winter returns...)

Io sto solo, e van fugaci
I am alone, and they-go fleeing
(I am alone, and all the songs)

colle nebbie decembrine tutti i canti,
with-the hazes of-December all the songs;
(and all the kisses of your lips)

tutti i baci delle labbra tue divine;
all the kisses of-the lip your divine;
(go fleeing with the December hazes;)

triste m'è la vita allor!
sad to-me-is the life then!
(then life is sad to me!)

Donaudy
Se volete un servidore...
If you-want a servant...

Se volete un servidore giovin, lindo e accostumato,
If you-want a servant young, neat and trained,
(If you want a young servant, neat and trained,)

pien di zelo e di vigore, non poltrone nè sbadato,
full of zeal and of vigor, not lazy nor careless,
(full of zeal and vigor, not lazy or careless,)

che sa farvi riverenza,
who knows-how to-make-himself bow,
(who knows how to bow, beautiful and ready,)

bello e pronto egli è già qui...
beautiful and ready he is already here...
(he is already here...)

Non ci vede, non ci sente, e,
Not they see, not they hear, and,
(One sees nothing, one hears nothing, and,)

per far le cose a modo, fa ben poco o quasi niente...
to do the things to custom, do well little or nearly nothing...
(does things according to custom, do a little well or nearly
nothing...)

Sol vi chiede per mercede uno squardo per semmana
Only to-you he-asks for reward a glance per week
(He only asks you for the reward of one glance per week)

e un sorriso a fin di mese...
and a smile at end of month...
(and a smile at the end of the month...)

Via, sì poco chi mai chiese nell'offrir sua servitù?
Go, so small who never asks of-the-offering his servitude?
(Go, so small is he who never asks but to offer his servitude?)

Se poi meglio un bel marito
If then better a beautiful husband
(If then you would prefer to receive)

gradireste avere a lato,
receive-it to-have with pleasure,
(a beautiful husband with pleasure,)

che non manchi sol d'udito,
who not you-want only to-listen,
(to whom you not only want to listen,)

ma anche d'occhi e d'odorato,
but also of-eyes and of-scent,
(but also of eyes, and of scent,)

tutto miele e complimenti,
all honey and compliments,
(all honey and compliments,)

bello e pronto egli è pur qui...
beautiful and ready he is likewise here...
(beautiful and ready, he is likewise here...)

Non borbotta, non impera, e,
Not he-mutters, not he-dominates, and,
(He doesn't mutter, he doesn't dominate, and,)

per far le cose a modo,
to-do the things to custom,
(does things according to custom,)

esce il giorno e torna a sera...
he-goes-out the day and he-returns at night...
(he goes out during the day and returns at night...)

Via, sposando, chi mai chiese questo solo e nulla più?
Go, marrying, who never asks this only and nothing more?
(Go, marrying, he who asks only this and nothing more?)

Donaudy
Se vuoi ch'io mora, amore, morrò...
If you-want that-I die, love, I-will-die...

Se vuoi ch'io mora, amore, morrò;
If you-want that-I die, love, I-will-die;
(If you want me to die, love, I will die;)

se vuoi ch'io fugga, fuggirò;
if you-want that-I flee, I-will-flee;
(if you want me to flee, I will flee;)

se vuoi ch'io pianga, piangerò le lacrime più amare;
if you-want that-I cry, I-will-cry the tears more bitter;
(if you want me to cry, I will cry the most bitter tears;)

ma lascia che io baccio le tue labbra dolci e tenere a baciare!
but let that I kiss the your lips sweet and tender to kiss!
(but let me kiss your sweet and tender lips!)

Mi vuoi dannar? mi dannerò;
Me you-want to-drive-mad? me I-will-go-mad;
(Do you want to drive me mad? I will go mad;)

vuoi darmi l'ali? volerò;
you-want to-give-me the-wings? I-will-fly;
(do you want to give me wings? I will fly away;)

mi vuoi tradir?
me you-want to-betray?
(you want to betray me?)

diventerò marito da ingannare;
I-will-become husband to deceive;
(I will become a partner in deception;)

Ma lascia che....
But let that....
(But let me kiss....)

Sorge il sol! Che fai tu?...
Rises the sun! What do you?...

Sorge il sol! Che fai tu?
Rises the sun! What do you?
(The sun rises! What are you doing?)

Che fai lassù?
What you-do up-there?
(What are you doing up there?)

Se dormi, svègliati: è primavera!
If you-sleep, wake-up: is spring!
(If you are sleeping, wake up: it is spring!)

Se vegli, lèvati: vieni a gioir!
If you-are-awake, rise-up: come-you to enjoy!
(If you are awake, get up: come enjoy yourself!)

E tempo venuto di correre ancor pei campi
Is time arrived to run still in-the fields
(The time has come to run through the fields)

stellanti di mille colori;
starry of thousand colors;
(bestarred with a thousand colors;)

di sciogliere canti, di cogliere fiori,
of to-loosen songs, of to-gather flowers,
(to loosen songs, to gather flowers,)

di ber lungo le rive,
to drink along the shores,
(to drink along the shores,)

d'avere nel cor le gioie d'amor!
to-have in-the heart the joys of-love!
(to have in your heart the joys of love!)

Vieni a gioir...Chè,
Come to enjoy...Because,
(Come and enjoy...Because,)

se tu non vieni, non sbocciano i fior.
if you not come, not they-blossom the flowers.
(if you don't come, the flowers will not blossom.)

Spirate pur, spirate...
Waft yet, waft...

Spirate pur, spirate attorno a lo mio bene,
Waft yet, waft around to the my beloved,
(Waft still, waft around to my beloved,)

aurette e v'accertate
little-breezes and yourselves-ascertain
(little breezes, and ascertain)

s'ella nel cor mi tiene,
if-she in-the heart me holds,
(if she holds me in her heart,)

Spirate, aurette!
Waft, little-breezes!
(Waft, little breezes!)

Se nel suo cor mi tiene,
If in-the her heart me she-holds,
(If she holds me in her heart,)

v'accertate aure beate,
yourselves-ascertain breezes blessed,
(ascertain, blessed breezes,)

aure lievi e beate!
breezes light and blessed!
(light and blessed breezes!)

Donaudy
Tempo è alfin di muover guerra...
Time is at-last tò induce war...

Tempo è alfin di muover guerra contro chi più ci tiranna,
Time is at-last to induce war against who more us oppresses,
(At last it is time to declare war against he who still opresses us,)

più c'illude e più c'inganna,
more us-deceives and more us-betrays,
(still deceives us and still betrays us,)

or fedele, or traditore...
now faithful, now traitor...
(now faithful, now traitor...)

Se un nemico abbiamo in terra, è l'Amor!
If an enemy we-have on earth, is the-Love!
(If we have an enemy on earth, it is Love!)

Basta avere un usbergo sul cuore:
Enough to-have a shield on-the heart:
(It is enough to have a shield on the heart:)

quello è il nostro tallone d'Achille...
that is the our tendon of-Achilles...
(that is our Achilles' tendon...)

Siam, del resto, più di mille, tutti pieni di vigore;
We-are, of-the rest, more than 1000, all full of vigor;
(We are, of all the rest, more than 1000, all full of vigor;)

sicchè certo l'Arcadore questa volta perirà!
thus certain the-Archer this time will-perish!
(thus certain this time that the Archer will perish!)

Mai crociata come questa fu più giusta,
Never he-crossed-himself like this was more justly,
(Never was he protected like this more justly,)

più fatale se salvarci può dal male,
more fatal if they-save could from-the harm.
(more fatally if they could save themselves from harm.)

onde tutti noi soffriamo...Su a cavallo!
whence all us suffer...On, to horse!
(whence we all suffer...On, to the horses!)

Lancia in resta! E voliam!
Spear in readiness! And we-fly!
(Spear in readiness! We fly!)

Ecco adesso in agguato sostiamo:
Here-is now in ambush we-sustain:
(Here now in ambush we wait:)

giunge Amore d'intorno saettando...Tutti fermi!
arrives Cupid of-around shooting...All stop!
(Cupid arrives shooting around...All stops!)

Solo quando egli è giunto noi sortiamo e prigion lo
Only when he is arrived we go-out and capture him
(Only when he has arrived do we go out and capture him)

dichiariamo...Ahi, che invece mi ferì!
we-declare...Ah, that instead to-me he-wounded!
(we declare...Ah, instead he wounded me!)

Donaudy
Tregua non ho...
Rest not I-have...

Tregua non ho nè sperar so più pace dacchè,
Rest not I-have nor to-hope to-know more peace since,
(I have no rest nor can I hope to know any peace since,)

rubando a due occhi di brace una favilla di loro pupilla,
stealing at two eyes of embers a spark of their pupils,
(stealing two embers of eyes, a spark of their pupils,)

bruciai di tal foco che, a stinguerlo un poco,
I-burned of so-much fire that, to fade-it a little,
(I burned with so much fire that, to lessen it a little,)

non potria bastare anch'esso il mare.
not could to-stop also-it the sea.
(the sea could not stop it.)

Potessi almeno a lei narrare quelle ond'io peno
Could-it at-least to her tell those of-which-I suffer
(Could it at least tell those regrets of love)

doglianze amare! Aurette, voi soltanto potreste dirle,
regrets to-love! Breezes, you only can tell-it
(by which I suffer! Breezes, only you can tell it,)

intanto, ch'io languo, ch'io brucio, ch'io moro d'amar.
meanwhile, that-I lanquish, that-I burn, that-I die of-love,
(meanwhile, I languish, I burn, I die of love,)

Per miglior sorte compagno vorria un serpe,
For better fate companion I-would-want a serpent,
(For a better fate I would prefer the companion of a serpent,)

un rospo o una mula restia,
a toad or a mule stubborn,
(a toad or a stubborn mule,)

anzi che questo mio amore funestro
rather that this my love funereal
(rather than this, my funereal love,)

che sì m'attanaglia,
that so me-tortures,
(that tortures me so,)

mi morde e travaglia ed è il mio tormento
me stings and afflicts and is the my torment
(stings and afflicts me and is my torment)

d'ogni momento.
of-every moment.
(at every moment.)

Vaghissima sembianza...
Very-vague appearance...

Vaghissima sembianza d'antica donna amata, chi, dunque,
Very-vague appearance of-former woman loved, who, then,
(Very vague image of a formerly loved woman, who, then,)

v'ha ritratta con tanta simiglianza
you-have withdrawn with so-much similarity
(you took away with so much similarity)

ch'io guardo, e parlo,
that-I see, and I-speak,
(that I see, and I speak)

e credo d'avervi a me davanti
and I-believe to-have-you to me in-front
(and I believe to have you before me)

come ai bei dì d'amor?
as to-the beautiful days of-love?
(as in the beautiful days of love?)

La cara rimembranza
The dear remembrance
(The dear remembrance)

che in cor me s'e destata sì ardente
which in heart to-me she-has woken-up so ardent
(which she has woken in my heart so ardently)

v'ha già fatta rinascer la speranza, che un bacio, un voto,
you-have already made revive the hope, that a kiss, a vow,
(you have already revived hope, that a kiss, a vow,)

un grido d'amore più non chiedo che a lei che muta è ognor.
a cry of-love more not I-ask that to her who mute is always.
(a cry of love I ask no more of her who is always mute.)

Venuto è l'aprile
Arrived is the-April

Venuto è l'Aprile tessendo ghirlande,
Arrived is the-April weaving garlands,
(April has arrived issuing forth its rains,)

e ninfe e silvani sul prato raunando.
and nymphs and sylvans in-the meadow play.
(and nymphs and sylvans play in the meadow.)

Accordan gli ontani i loro strumenti
Tune the alders the their instruments
(The alder trees tune their instruments)

e ai primi concenti del vento
and at-the first melodies of-the wind
(and begin the dance at the first melodies)

fra i rami comincia la danza.
between the branches begin the dance.
(of the wind between the branches.)

Prima un fauno s'avanza...La sua ninfa lo mira...
First a faun himself-advances...The his nymph him sees...
(First a faun advances...His nymph sees him...)

Sospira...E volano insiem!
Breathes...And they-fly-away together!
(Breathes...And they fly away together!)

Folleggian le coppie tra i fonti e le rive,
Frolic the couple among the fountains and the rivers,
(The pair frolics among the fountains and the rivers,)

e poi nelle selve scompaion furtive...
and then in-the woods disappear secretly...
(and then disappear secretly into the woods...)

Ma Clori, che intanto gelosa è di Nice,
But Clori, who meanwhile jealous is in Nice,
(But Clori, who, jealous, is meanwhile in Nice,)

aspetta infelice e sola, nel pianto, che cessi la danza.
awaits unhappy and alone, in-the tears, which ends the dance.
(unhappy and alone waits, in her tears, which ends the dance.)

Ma un pastore s'avanza...
Ah a shepherd himself-advances...
(Ah, a shepherd advances...)

e già Clori lo mira...
and already Clori him sees...
(and already Clori sees him...)

Sospira...E volano insiem!
Breathes...And they-fly-away together!
(Breathes...And they fly away together!)

Vorrei poterti odiare...
I-would-like to-be-able-you to-hate...

Vorrei poterti odiare,
I-would-like to-be-able-you to-hate,
(I would like to be able to hate you,)

ma troppo schiavo ho il cor.
but too-much slave I-have the heart.
(but my heart is too much a slave)

Ripenso alle tante promesse mendaci,
I-recall to-the so-many promises false,
(I recall so many false promises,)

ai lunghi tormenti durati sin qui,
to-the long torments you-continue until now,
(the long torments you continue until now,)

eppur ti ricopro le labbra di baci,
and-yet to-you I-recover the lips of kisses,
(and yet your lips I cover again with kisses,)

ti stringo al mio core che tanto soffrì,
to-you I-press to-the my heart which so-much it-suffered,
(I press you to my heart which suffered so much,)

che sanguina e chiede pietà al suo dolor.
that it-bleeds and it-asks pity for-the its sorrow.
(that it bleeds and asks pity for its sorrow.)

Donizetti
Ah! rammenta, o bella Irene
Ah! remember, o beautiful Irene

Ah rammenta, o bella Irene,
Ah remember, oh beautiful Irene,
(Ah remember, oh beautiful Irene,)

che giurasti a me costanza.
that promised-you to me constancy.
(that you promised constancy to me.)

Ah ritorna, amato bene, ah! ritorna al primo amor,
Ah return, loved well, ah! return to-the first love,
(Ah return, beloved, ah! return to the first love,)

qual conforto, oh! Dio, m'avanza,
some comfort, oh! God, me-it-advances,
(some comfort, oh! God, I grow older,)

chi sarà la mia speranza?
who will-be the my hope?
(who will be my hope?)

Per chi viver più degg'io, se più mio non è quel cor,
For who to-live more must-I, if more my not is that heart,
(For whom must I live longer, if that heart is no longer mine,)

Chi mai di questo core saprà le vie secrete,
Who never of that heart will-know the ways secret,
(Who ever will know the secret ways of that heart,)

se voi non le sapete, begl'occhi del mio ben,
if you not it to-know, beautiful-eyes of-the my beloved,
(if you do not know it, beautiful eyes of my beloved,)

voi che dal primo istante, quando divenni amante,
you that of-the first instant, when having-become loving,
(you who at the first instant, when being in love,)

il mio nascosto foco mi conosceste in sen.
the my hidden fire to-me knew in breast.
(knew the hidden fire in my breast.)

A Mezzanotte
At Midnight

Quando notte sarà oscura
When night will-be dark
(When night is dark)

e le stelle in ciel vedrai,
and the stars in heaven you-will-see,
(and in heaven you will see stars,)

cheto cheto mi verrai nel mio asilo a ritrovar.
quiet quiet to-me you-will-come in-the my shelter to re-find.
(quietly you will come into my shelter to find me again.)

Nel silenzio della notte dent'all'umile mio tetto,
In-the silence of-the night inside-to-the-humble my roof,
(In the silence of the night inside under my humble roof,)

vieni puro, o mio diletto, la tua ninfa a consolar:
come pure, oh my delight, the your nymph to console:
(come chaste, oh my delight to console your nymph:)

canta pur la tua canzone, ch'io t'attendo sul balcone, ah!
sing now the your song, that-I you-await on-the balcony, ah!
(sing your song now, that I await you on the balcony, ah!)

Ma non debbo a te soltanto aprir l'uscio a notte bruna;
But not I-must to you only to-open the-door at night dark;
(But I must not open the door to you only at night;)

coprirebbesi la luna, vereconda in suo pudor.
cover-yourself the moon, shy in your bashfulness.
(cover yourself, moon, shy in your bashfulness.)

Noi due soli non saremo, verecondia non consente;
Us two alone not are, modesty not consents;
(We two are not alone, modesty does not consent to that)

vuo che un terzo sia presente, e quel terzo sia l'amor:
you-wish that a third is present, and that third is the-love:
(you know a third is present, and that third is love:)

canta...io t'attendo a mezzanotte,
sing...I you-await at midnight,
(sing...I await you at midnight,)

cheto cheto ne verrai,
quiet quiet nor you-will-come,
(quietly or you will not come,)

noi due soli non saremo no no no vuo
us two alone not are no no no you-wish
(we two are not alone no no no you know)

che il terzo sia l'amor. Ah!
that the third is the-love. Ah!
(that the third is love. Ah!)

Amore e morte
Love and death

Odi d'un uom che muore, odi l'estremo suon
Hear of-a man who is-dying, hear the last sound
(Hear a man who is dying, hear his last sound)

quest'appassito fiore ti lascio Elvira in don.
that-faded flower to-you I-leave Elvira as gift.
(I leave this faded flower to you Elvira as a gift.)

Quanto prezioso ei sia.
How precious he is.
(How precious he is.)

Tu dei saperlo appien nel di che fosti mia
You must know-it fully as-soon-as day that you-were mine
(You must have known it as soon as the day you were mine)

te lo involai dal sen.
to-you it I-stole from-the breast.
(from your breast I stole it.)

Simbolo allor d'affetto or pegno di dolor
Symbol then of-affection now pledge of pain
(Then a symbol of affection now a pledge of pain)

torna a posarti in petto questo appassito fior
returns to place-you in breast this faded flower
(return to place this faded flower on your breast)

e avrai nel cor scolpito, se duro il cor
and you-will-have in-the heart carved, if hard the heart
(and you will have carved in your heart, if it was not)

non è come ti fu rapito come ritorna a te.
not is like from-you was taken like returns to you.
(hard like when it was taken from you.)

Donizetti
Che cangi tempra
What you-change time

Che cangi tempra mai più non spero
What you-change time never more not I-hope
(I no longer hope that you change)

quel cor macchato d'infedelta.
that heart spotted of-infidelity.
(your spotted heart of infidelity.)

Io dirò sempre, nel mio pensiero,
I will-say always, in-the my thought,
(I will always say, in my thoughts,)

chi m'ha ingannato m'ingannerà.
who me-you-have deceived me-you-will-deceive.
(me, whom you have deceived, you will deceive again.)

Depuis q'une autre a su te plaire
Since that-an other has known you to please

Depuis q'une autre a su te plaire
Since that-an other has known you to-please
(Since when another has known how to please you)

chaque jour me voit deperir.
every day me it-sees to-decline.
(every day sees me decline.)

Quand Malvina ne t'est plus chère
When Malvina not you-is more dear
(When Malvina is no longer dear to you,)

Malvina ne veut que mourir.
Malvina not wants but to-die.
(Malvina wants only to die.)

Pourtant sa faible voix t'implore
However her feeble voice you-implores
(However, her feeble voice implores you,)

non pour réclamer ton amour,
not to crave your love,
(not to crave your love,)

non, non, non, mais avant de perdre le jour pour te voir
no, no, no, but before of losing the day for you-to-see
(no, no, no, but to see you once more before the day is lost.)

une fois encore. Hâte toi, le trépas s'avance;
one time again. Haste you, the death it-advances;
(Hurry yourself, death advances;)

viens voir celle qui t'adorait mourir sur un lit
come to-see that-one who you-adored to-die on a bed
(come to see that one who adored you die on a bed)

de souffrance d'amour, de honte et de regret.
of suffering of-love, of shame and of regret.
(suffering from love, from shame and regret.)

Mais ce n'est point son agonie
But that neither-is not-at-all her agony
(But that not-is not-at-all of her agony)

ni la mort empreinte
nor the death imprinted
(nor death imprinted)

en ses traits, non, non, non, ah! qui te diront
on her features, no, no, no, ah! who you will-tell
(on her features, no, no, no, ah! never tell)

que pour jamais Malvina va perdre la vie.
that for never Malvina goes to-lose the life.
(for whom Malvina loses her life.)

Mais si lanquissante, abattue je ne sais plus
But if languishing, depressed I not know more
(But if depressed and languishing I can no longer)

compter tes pas quand tu paraîtras à ma vue,
to-count your steps when you will-appear to my view,
(count your steps when you appear in my view,)

si tout mon corps ne frémit pas,
if all my body not quivers not,
(if all my body does not quiver,)

si mon regard ne peut te suivre,
if my glance not can you to-follow,
(if my glance cannot follow you,)

si ma voix ne peut te nommer,
if my voice not can you to-name,
(if my voice cannot name you,)

ah! si mon coeur a cessé d'aimer
ah! if my heart has ceased of-loving
(ah! if my heart has ceased loving)

alors j'aurai cessé de vivre.
then I-will-have ceased of-living.
(then I will have ceased living.)

Donizetti
E morta
Is dead

Morta e ieri ancor, qui vagheggiai,
Dead and yesterday still, who I-longed-for,
(Dead and still yesterday, she who I longed for,)

il lampeggiar di due bei rai!
the lightening of two beautiful rays!
(the light of two beautiful eyes!)

Oh! l'amor mio, dove fuggì?
Oh! the-love my, where you-flown?
(Oh! my love, where have you gone?)

morte spietata me lo rapì,
death ruthless to-me it carries-off,
(death, ruthless to me, carries it off,)

morta e ier la vagheggiai,
dead and yesterday it I-longed-for,
(dead, and yesterday I longed for it,)

morta, morta! Più non ascolta nè i giuramenti,
dead, dead! More not listen neither the oaths,
(dead, dead! Don't listen anymore neither to my oaths,)

nè il flebil suono de' miei lamenti, ella è morta.
nor the feeble sound of-the my laments, she is dead.
(nor the feeble sound of my laments, she is dead.)

Or vive un angiol di più nel ciel.
Now lives an angel of more in-the heaven.
(Now another angel lives in heaven.)

Ieri ancor col suo sospir
Yesterday still with-the its sigh
(Yesterday Paradise with its sigh)

il paradiso sembrommi aprir:
the paradise it-seemed-to-me to-open:
(seemed to open to me:)

fu la sua voce canto seren,
was the her voice singing serene,
(her voice was serenely singing,)

che mi calmava l'affanno in sen,
that to-me calmed the-pang in breast,
(that calmed the pang in my breast,)

morta! e ieri ancora stendea la mano al poverello
dead! and yesterday still extended the hand to-the poor-man
(dead! and still yesterday was a mother who tearfully prayed)

con volto umano, era una madre che lagrimosa il ciel
with face human, was a mother who tearfully the heaven
(extended her hand to the poor man with a human face)

pregava per la pietosa morta, morta!
prayed for the pitious dead, dead!
(and prayed for the pitious dead, dead!)

Donizetti
Eterno Amore e fe
Eternal Love and faith

Eterno Amore e fe, ti giuro umile ai pie,
Eternal Love and faith, to-you I-pledge humbly at-the feet,
(Eternal Love and faith, I pledge humbly at your feet,)

ti giuro eterna fe, presente Iddio,
to-you I-pledge eternal faith, present God,
(I pledge to you eternal faith, in the presence of God,)

ti giuro amor, ti giuro fe, presente Iddio.
to-you I-pledge love, to-you I-pledge faith, present God.
(I pledge love to you, I pledge faith to you, in the presence of
God.)

Viver, morir per te è il solo ben
To-live, to-die for you is the only good
(To live, to die for you is the only good)

che a me dal ciel desio.
that to me of-the heaven desires.
(that heaven desires of me.)

Il barcaiolo
The boatman

Voga, voga, il vento tace, pura è l'onde, il ciel sereno,
Row, row, the wind silent, pure is the-wave, the sky serene,
(Row, row, silent wind, the wave is pure, the sky serene,)

solo un alito di pace par che allegri è cielo e mar:
alone a breeze of peace it-seems that cheerful is sky and sea:
(alone a breeze of peace seems that the sky and sea are
cheerful:)

voga, voga, o marinar.
row, row, o sailor.
(row, row, o sailor.)

Or che tutto a noi sorride in sì tenero momento,
Now that everything to us smiles in such tender moment,
(Now that everything smiles at us in such a tender moment,)

all'ebbrezza del contento voglio l'alme abbandonar,
to-the-elation of-the happiness I-want the-souls to-abandon,
(I want souls to abandon themselves to the elation of
happiness,)

voga, voga, o marinar, o marinar.
row, row, oh sailor, oh sailor,
(row, row, oh sailor, oh sailor,)

Che se infiera la tempesta, e ambidue ne tragge a morte,
That if rages the storm, and both of-us it-drags to death,
(If the storm rages, and drags both of us to death,)

sarà lieta la mia sorte, al tuo fianco vuò spirar:
will-be happy the my fate, at-the your side I-want to-expire:
(happy will be my fate, I want to expire at your side:)

voga, voga, o marinar, o marinar.
row, row, oh sailor, oh sailor.
(row, row, oh sailor, oh sailor.)

Donizetti
Il mio ben m'abbandono
The my beloved me-has-abandoned

Il mio ben m'abbandono,
The my beloved me-has-abandoned,
(My beloved has abandoned me,)

giusto ciel come vivrò?
just heaven how will-I-live?
(just heaven, how will I live?)

Morirò di dolor, crudo amor.
I-will-die of sorrow, cruel love.
(I will die of sorrow, cruel love.)

Il pescatore
The Fisherman

Era l'ora che i cieli lente
Was the-hour that the skies slow
(It was the hour when the slow moving clouds)

mandan l'ombre sfumate, e ch'ogni istante, tacito,
send the-shades vague, and that-each instant, silent,
(were sending vague shadows, and each instant, silent,)

fuggente, sul fronte della sera,
fleeting, on-the face of-the evening,
(fleeting, at dusk,)

ingenuo e puro spande un velo più scuro.
naive and pure spread a veil more dark.
(naively and purely spread a darker veil.)

Sovra un limpido lago un batteliero col suo battel leggero
On a limpid lake a boatman with-the his boat light
(On a limpid lake a boatman with his light boat)

tracciava un solco che vedea svanir siccome il sovvenir
traced a trail that he-saw disappearing like the remembrance
(traced a trail that he was disappearing like the remembrance)

dei dì che furo.
of-the days which were.
(of days which were.)

E giovane e leggiadro il pescatore
Is young and handsome the fisherman
(The fisherman is young and handsome)

e deliba l'incanto d'un lieto dì
and enjoys the-enchantment of-a happy day
(and enjoys the enchantment of a happy day)

ne' sogni di speranza.
in-the dreams of hope.
(in his dreams of hope.)

E canta e tutto tace, che il suo canto
And he-sings and everything quiets, that the his singing
(And he sings and everything is quiet, because his singing)

è il canto dell'amor, si, dell'amore.
is the singing of-the-love, yes, of-the-love.
(is the singing of love, yes, of love.)

Oh! vent'anni giungeste,
Oh! twenty-years you-reached,
(Oh! you have reached age twenty,)

nè un core del mio core
neither a heart of-the my heart
(neither a heart of my heart)

la voce ha sentita, nè la rosa sul seno appassita
the voice has heard, nor the rose on-the breast withered
(has heard the voice, nor the rose on my withered breast)

una vergine a sera mi diè.
a virgin at evening me gave.
(gave me a virgin at evening.)

La mia barca abbandona la riva senza un caro sussurro,
The my boat abandons the shore without a dear whisper,
(My boat leaves the shore without a dear whisper,)

un addio, senza un guardo una voce che a Dio impolrasse
a goodbye, without a look a voice which to God implores
a goodbye, without a look a voice implores God for)

un sospiro per me. Ahi, ahimè! ma tace, ascolta!
a sigh for me. Ah, alas! but silent, listen!
(a sigh on me. Ah, alas! but silently, listen!)

al canto suo dall'onde una voce risponde, la spranza
to-the song his from-the-waves a voice answers, the smile
(to his song from the waves a voice answers, the smile)

sul labbro gli ridea e la voce d'amor dicea così:
on-the lips to-him laughed and the voice of-love said like-
this:
(on his lips laughed at him and the voice of love said this:)

A me giunse il tuo lamento, mi feri quel caro accento.
To me reached the your lament, me wounded that dear stress,
(Your lament reached me, that dear word wounded me,)

Son la dea di questo lago, il mio viso è puro e vago;
I-am the Goddess of this lake, the my face is pure and pretty;
(I am the Goddess of this lake, my face is pure and pretty;)

giovinetto pescator, per te palpito d'amor, per te.
little-young fisherman, for you I-palpitate of-love, for you.
(young little fisherman, for you I tremble of love, for you.)

Ah! non morrà la mia bellezza, non morrà tuo giovinezza;
Ah! not will-die the my beauty, not will-die your youth;
(Ah! my beauty will not die, your youth will not die;)

sovra un trono di corallo, sotto un cielo di cristallo, vieni,
on a throne of coral, under a sky of crystal, come,
(on a throne of coral, under a sky of crystal, come,)

pescatore, vieni al bacio dell'amor. Tacque e
fisherman, come to-the kiss of-the-love. Silent and
(fisherman, come to the kiss of your love. Silently and)

s'udia sul lago e sulla sponda un mesto mormorio
one-heard on-the lake and on-the bank a sad murmur
(one heard on the lake and on the bank a sad murmur)

che affievoliva fino alla riva
which weakened as-far to-the shore
(which softened as far as the shore,)

urtando d'onda in onda,
bubbling from-wave to wave,
(bubbling from wave to wave,)

sino alla riva.
up to-the shore.
(up to the shore.)

E quando l'alba cominciò a spuntare del pescator,
And when the-daybreak began to appear of-the fisherman,
(And when daybreak began to appear to the fisherman,)

la folla costernata,
the crowd dismayed,
(the dismayed crowd,)

la barca abbandonata vide errare abbandonata.
the boat abandoned it-was-seen wandering abandoned.
(the abandoned boat was seen wandereing abandoned.)

Il sospiro
The sigh

Donna infelice, stanca d'amore,
Woman unfaithful, tired of-love,
(Unfaithful woman, tired of love,)

l'eterno sonno chiedi all'avel?
the-eternal sleep you-ask to-the-grave?
(you ask for the eternal sleep of the grave?)

Deh! non rammenti, che qui v'è un core che,
Ah! not you-recall, that here to-you-is a heart that,
(Ah! don't you recall, that here is a heart that,)

te perduta, perduto ha il ciel?
of-you lost, lost it-has the heaven?
(without you, it has lost heaven?)

L'Eden ridente quaggiù la speme
The-Eden laughing down-here the hopes
(Eden laughing down here can give us renewed hopes)

rinnovellata ci può donar
renewed us can to-give If you-implore death,
(If you implore death, we will die together,)

Se implori morte, moriamo insieme, angiol mio caro,
we-will-die together, angel my dear,
(my dear angel,)

non mi lasciar.
not me to-leave.
(do not leave me.)

Ma se ricusi ch'or teco stretto
But if you-refuse that-now you-with confined
(But if you refuse and now must ascend)

nel riso eterno debba salir,
in-the smile eternal must to-ascend,
(confined in your eternal smile,)

onde la vita mi resti
by-which the life me rests
(on which the life in my breast life rests)

in petto, dammi l'estremo caldo sospir.
in breast, give-me the-last warm sigh.
(give me your last warm sigh.)

L'amor funesto
The-love deadly

Più che non ama un angelo, t'amai nel mio deliro,
More that not loves an angel, you-I-loved in-the my rapture,
(An angel loves no more, you I loved in my rapture,)

mi fusi nel tuo spirito, vissi nel tuo respiro,
to-me fused in-the your spirit, I-lived in-the your breath,
(I joined myself in your spirit, I lived in your breath,)

ma un core senza palpiti, un giuro senza fè,
but a heart without palpitations, an oath without faith,
(but a heart without palpitations, an oath without faith,)

un riso senza lagrime, donna, tu desti a me, ah!
a smile without tears, woman, you gave to me, ah!
(a smile without tears, woman, you gave to me, ah!)

Addio, lontano è il tumulo, che accoglierà quest'ossa,
Goodbye, far-away is the tomb, that will-receive these-bones,
(Goodbye, the tomb is far away, that will receive these
bones,)

ne resterà pei gemiti la traccia della fossa
of-it will-rest in-the moans the footsteps of-the grave
(the moans of the footsteps of the grave will rest in it)

l'angiol tu fosti e il demone de' miei consunti dì,
the-angel you were and the demon of my wasted days,
(you were my angel and the demon of my wasted days,)

oh! donna, addio, ah!
oh! woman, goodbye, ah!
(oh! woman, goodbye, ah!)

T'amo, dicesti a un misero, ed egli ne morì.
You-I-love, you-told to a mystery, and he of-it died.
(I love you, you told a mystery, and of it he died.)

Donizetti
L'amor mio
The-love my

Amo, sì, ma l'amor mio,
I-love, yes, but the-love my,
(I love, yes, but my love,)

niun fra voi comprender può;
no-one among you comprehends can;
(no one among you can comprehend;)

solo in cielo è noto a Dio,
alone in heaven is known to God,
(in heaven only God knows,)

sulla terra io sola il sò.
on-the earth I alone the know.
(on earth I alone know.)

Ei mi vive in fondo al core,
He me lives in base to-the heart,
(He lives in the bottom of my heart,)

qual profumo in sen d'un fiore,
what perfume in breast of-a flower,
(what a flower's perfume in my breast,)

che non anco s'esalò.
that not also it emitted.
(that it also emitted.)

Nei conviti, nelle feste, fra beltade e gioventù,
In-the banquets, in-the festivals, amidst beauty and youth,
(In the banquets, in the festivals, amidst beauty and youth,)

a cercarlo invan torreste,
to search-for-it in vain to-take it,
(to search for love in vain, to take it,)

non è cosa di quaggiù,
not is like-that of down-here,
(is not like that down here,)

è un immago tutta pura, è un sorriso di natura,
is an image all pure, is a smile of nature,
(here is an image all pure, here is a smile of nature,)

è una luce di virtù. Dov'ei sia, qual'è il suo nome,
is a light of virtue. Where-he is, what-is the his name,
(here is a light of virtue. Where he is, what his name is,)

un arcano, è pur per me, ma dipinto io non so come,
a mystery, and pure for me, but painting I not know how,
(a mystery, and pure for me, but I don't know how to
describe it,)

pien di vita in seno ei m'è.
full of life in breast he me-is.
(he is full of life in my breast.)

Nè sembianze fra mortali,
Neither resemblances among mortals,
(Neither resemblances among mortals,)

mai non vidi, a quelle uguali
never not lived, to that equal
(never having lived, equals)

che il mio cor vagheggia in sè.
that the my heart longs-for in itself.
(that which my heart itself longs for.)

Ah! vagheggia in sè.
Ah! longs-for in itself.
(Ah! itself longs for.)

(See Donizetti - Meine Liebe)

Donizetti
La conocchia
The distaff

Quann'a lo bello mio voglio parlare,
When-to the beautiful-one my I-want to-speak,
(When I want to talk to my beautiful one,)

ca spiso me ne vene lu golio,
I often to-me of-it comes the wish,
(a wish often comes to me,)

a la fenesta me mett'a finlare,
to the window my I-put-to spin,
(I put myself by the window to spin,)

quann'a lo bello mio voglio parlare,
when-to the beautiful-one my I-want to-speak,
(when I want to talk to my beautiful one,)

quann'isso passa, pò rompo lo filo e co na grazia
when-he passes, then I-break the thread and with a grace
(I then break my thread and with grace)

me mett' a priare, bello,
me I-put to pray, beautiful-one,
(when he passes, I begin to pray, beautiful one,)

peccarità, proitemillo, isso lu piglia e io lo stò
sin, prohibit-me-it, he it takes and I him stay
(sin, keep me from it, he takes it away and stay)

a guradare, e accosì me ne vao mpilo, ajemè!
to watch, and this-way my it go away, poor-me!
(watching him, and thus take away my sin, alas!)

La correspondance amoureuse
The corresponence amorous

Billets chéris, interprètes de l'âme,
Notes dear, interpreters of the-soul,
(Dear letters, interpreters of my soul,)

je n'ose pas vous garder plus longtemps;
I not-dare not you to-see more longtime;
(I dare not see you any longer;)

né de ses feux perissez dans la flamme j'ai peur de vous
born of these fires perish in the flame I-have fear of you
(born of these fires, perish in flame, I fear you,)

indiscrets confidents, c'en est donc fait tous ces écrits
indiscrete confidantes, that-it is then done all these writings
(indiscrete confidantes, that all these writings)

si tendres, ne seront plus, helas! qu'un peu de cendres.
so tender, not will-be more, alas! but-a little of ashes.
(so tender have been made, be no more, alas! but a few ashes.)

Brulez! brulez! gages d'amour,
Burn! burn! pledges of-love,
(Burn! burn! pledges of love,)

vous serez là gravés toujours.
you will-be there engraved always.
(you will be engraved there always.)

Je veux encor palpitante,
I want still palpitating,
(I still want, palpitating,)

et revie de leur nectar m'enivrer
and re-live of their nectar me-to-intoxicate
(to relive their nectar and to intoxicate myself)

une fois: de flot en flot je remonte ma vie;
one time: of wave by wave I remount my life;
(once more: surge by surge I regain my life;)

dans chaque mot je retrouve sa voix.
in every word I refind your voice.
(in every word I refind your voice.)

Billets chéris, mon beau trésor, ma gloire,
Notes dear, my beautiful treasure, my glory,
(Dear letters, my beautiful treasure, my glory,)

avant l'adieu passez dans ma memoire.
before the-goodbye pass in my memory.
(pass through my memory before the goodbye.)

Quand il saura le dernier sacrifice pour l'adoucir,
When he will-know the last sacrifice to her-soften,
(When he will know the last sacrifice to soften her,)

qu'il me plaigne du moins, billets chéris,
that-it me pities of-the less, notes dear,
(that it pities me less, dear letters,)

que le sort s'accomplisse,
that the fate itself-completed,
(that fate completed itself,)

disparaissez sans pitié sans témoins.
disappear without pity, without witnesses.
(disappear without pity, without witnesses.)

Ah! les transports de l'étranger qui m'aime,
Ah! the raptures of the-foreigner who me-loves,
(Ah! the raptures of the foreigner who loves me,)

qu'ils n'aillent point s'évanouir,
that-they not-may-go never themselves-to-disappear,
(may you raptures never disappear,)

de même, brulez! brulez! gages d'amour,
of same, burn! burn! notes of-love,
(all the same, burn! burn! love letters,)

mais dans son coeur vivez toujours.
but in his heart live always.
(but live in his heart always.)

(See Donizetti - La corrispondenza amorosa)

Donizetti
La corrispondenza amorosa
The correspondence amorous

Cifre d'amor, sol conforto del core,
Signs of-love, only comfort of-the heart,
(Signs of love, only comfort of my heart,)

non v'oso più nel mio seno occultar;
not you-dare more in-the my breast to-hide;
(don't dare to hide any longer in my breast;)

figlie d'amor, sol vi danna l'amore,
daughters of-love, only you damage the-love,
(daughters of-love, only you damage love,)

potreste voi la sua fiamma svelar,
could you the your flame to-reveal,
(if you could only reveal your flame,)

o care cifre affettuose e tenere, voi non sarete più
o dear signs affectionate and tender, you not will-be more
(o dear affectionate and tender signs, you will not be more)

che poca cenere. Ardete pur, pegni d'amor,
than little ashes. You-burn now, pledges of-love,
(than little ashes. Burn now, pledges of love,)

voi qui sarete scolpiti ognor.
you who will-be carved always.
(you who will be always carved in my heart.)

Io voglio ancor palpitante
I wish again palpitating
(Palpitating and blessed)

e beata inebbriarmi un'istante d'amor:
and blessed make-elated-me an-insant of-love:
(I want again to be elated in an instant of love:)

e penso al ben della vita passata
and I-think to-the good of-the life passed
(and I think of the goodness of the past life,)

ed odo il suon della sua voce ancor.
and I-hear the sound of-the your voice still.
(and I still hear the sound of your voice,)

O care cifre, mia gioia, mia gloria,
O dear signs, my joy, my glory,
(O dear signs, my joy, my glory,)

grata terrò nel cor di voi memoria.
grateful I-will-hold in-the heart of you memory.
(I will gratefully hold your memory in my heart.)

Quand'ei saprà sì crudel sagrifizio, di pianto il ciglio allor
When-he will-be so cruel sacrifice, of tears the eyebrow then
(When he will be so cruelly sacrificed, tears will then moisten)

ci bagnerà, cifre d'amor,
them will-moisten, signs of-love,
(my eyebrows, signs of love,)

il destin reo si compia,
the destiny guilty itself content,
(guilty destiny, itself content,)

non visti ardete via senza pietà.
not you-saw ardent you-go without pity.
(not ardently you saw, you destiny, go on without pity.)

Deh! quell'amor con che il mio ben m'adora
Ah! that-love with which the my beloved me-adores
(Ah! that love with which my beloved adores me)

siccome poi non isvanisca o mora.
as then not vanishes or dies.
(then does not vanish or die.)

(See Donizetti - La correspondance amoureuse)

Donizetti
La dernière nuit d'un novice
The last night of-a novice

(Le novice:)   (The novice:)

Demain, quand sonnera l'heure de la prière,
Tomorrow, when will-sound the-hour of the prayer,
(Tomorrow, when the hour of prayer sounds,)

je franchirai les marches de l'autel.
I will-leap the steps of the-altar.
(I will leap the altar steps.)

Sur moi du ciel descendrà la lumière;
On me of-the heaven will-descend the light;
(The light of heaven will descend on me;)

à Dieu je vais m'unir par un voeu solennel.
to God I go me-to-unite by a vow solemn.
(I go to be united with God by a solemn vow.)

Jusqu'à demain attendre encore!
Until tomorrow to-wait still!
(I still wait for tomorrow!)

nuit trop lente, presse ton cours;
night too slow, press your flight;
(slow night, press your flight;)

hâte-toi: fais place à l'aurore du plus beau
hasten-you: make place for the-morning of-the most beautiful
(Hurry: make room for the loveliest morning)

de mes plus beaux jours.
of my most beautiful days.
(of my most beautiful days.)

Et toi descends, ô mon bon ange,
And you descend, oh my good angel,
(And descend, oh my good angel,)

viens me dire dans mon sommeil cette inéfable paix,
come me to-say in my sleep that inexpressable peace,
(tell me in my sleep that inexpressable peace,)

ce bonheur sans melange qui m'attend à mon réveil.
that goodness without mix which me-awaits at my waking.
(that only goodness awaits me at my waking.)

(Le malin esprit:)   (The evil spirit:)

Qu'elle espérance mensongère fascine et tes sens, et ton coeur?
What hope false fascinates and your senses, and your heart?
(What false hope fascinates you and your senses, and your
heart?)

Quoi! dans l'isolement,
What! in the-isolation,
(What! alone,)

le jeûne et la prière tu prétends trouver le bonheur?
the young and the prayer you pretend to-find the happiness?
(you pretend to find youth and prayer, and you pretend)

Ah! tu ne connais pas les plaisirs de la vie,
Ah! you not understand not the pleasures of the life,
(to find happiness?   Ah! you don't understand life's
pleasures,)

ces trèsors, ces douceurs qu'ici bas nous goûtons.
these treasures, these sweetnesses that-here below we taste.
(these treasures, these sweetnesses that we taste down here.)

Dieu nous les a donnés dans sa grâce infinie;
God us them has given in his grace infinite;
(God has given them to us in his infinite grace;)

n'est ce pas l'outrager, que mépriser ses dons?
not-is that not the-outrage, that to-despise these gifts?
(Is it not an outrage to dispise these gifts?)

Arrête, arrête, il en est temps; le monde t'appelle;
Stop, stop, the of-it is time; the world you-calls;
(Stop, stop, there is still time; the world calls you;)

suis-moi, suis-moi, viens, viens, ah! viens, viens!
follow-me, follow-me, come, come, ah! come, come!
(follow me, follow me, come, come, ah! come, come!)

(Le novice:) (The novice:)

Qu'ai-je entendu? où conduit-on mes pas?
What-have-I heard? where guides them my steps?
(What did I hear? where are my steps being guided?)

Non! ce n'etait qu'un rêve...ô mon ange fidèle,
No! that not-was but-a dream...oh my angel faithful,
(No! it was but a dream...oh my faithful angel.)

descendez, descendez;
descend, descend;
(descend, descend;)

ne me quittez pas jusqu'à l'aube nouvelle,
not me leave not until the-dawn new,
(don't leave me before dawn,)

mon bon ange, ne me quittez pas, non, descendez.
my good angel, not me leave not, no, descend.
(my good angel, don't leave me, no, descend.)

Angelus dei, qui custos es meus,
Angel God, who guardian is my,
(Angel of God, who is my guardian,)

me tibi commissum pieta.
me to-you has come have-pity.
(have pity on me who has come to you.)

(Le malin esprit:)   (The evil spirit:)

Regarde là, ces deux jeunes époux:
Look there, those two young spouses:
(Look there, that young couple:)

comme il est tendre, comme elle est heureuse,
how he is tender, how she is happy,
(how tender he is, how happy she is,)

vois leurs regards, entends ces mots si doux,
see their gazes, hear those words so sweet,
(see their gazes, hear those words so sweet,)

qu'échange leur bouche amoureuse, et cet enfant,
that-exchange their mouth loving, and that baby,
(that their loving mouths exchange, and that baby,)

beau comme un chérubin, dont le sourire appelle une caresse;
beautiful like a cherubim, in the smile calls a caress;
(like a beautiful cherubim, with a caress in its smile;)

c'est leur trésor, le fruit de leur hymen,
that-is their treasure, the fruit of their marriage,
(that is their treasure, the fruit of their marriage,)

oui cet enfant c'est leur trésor,
yes that infant that-is their treasure,
(yes, that baby is their treasure,)

le fruit de leur hymen et son amour
the fruit of their marriage and their love
(the fruit of their marriage and their love)

a doublé leur tendresse,
has doubled their tenderness,
(has doubled their tenderness,)

oui cet enfant a doublé leur tendresse.
yes that infant has doubled their tenderness.
(yes that baby has doubled their tenderness.)

Quels plaisirs purs! Ils sont dignes de toi!
What pleasures pure! They are worthy of you!
(What pure pleasures! They are worthy of you!)

viens les goûter, viens, viens, viens, viens.
come them to-taste, come, come, come, come.
(come taste them, come, come, come, come.)

(Le novice:)   (The novice:)

Ah! pitié de moi, mon Dieu, pitié!
Ah! pity of me, my God, pity!
(Ah! have pity on me, my God, have pity!)

mais ce n'était qu'un rêve: grâce à toi, mon ange,
but that not-was that-a dream: grace to you, my angel,
(but that was not a dream: grace to you, my angel,)

grâce à toi il s'achève, merci, merci:
grace to you the itself-stops, thank-you, thank-you:
(grace comes to you, thank you, thank you:)

grâce à toi, mon bon ange,
grace to you, my beautiful angel,
(grace to you, my beautiful angel,)

merci tu calmes mon émoi, merci,
thank-you you calm my emotion, thank-you,
(thank you for calming my fear, thank you,)

merci mon bon ange, merci.
thank-you my beautiful angel, thank-you.
(thank you my beautiful angel, thank you.)

Angelus Dei, qui custoses meus, me tibi commissum....
Angel God, who guardian my, me to-you has-come
(Angel of God, who is my guardian, I have come to you....)

(Le malin esprit:)   (The evil spirit:)

Cette jeune fille où va-t-elle? le teint pâle,
That young girl where goes-you-she? the tint pale,
(Where is that young girl going? the pale tint,)

les yeux en pleurs? dans sa tristesse ah!
the eyes in tears? in her sadness, ah!
(the crying eyes? in her sadness, ah!)

qu'elle est belle! mais qui peut causer ses douleurs!
that-she is beautiful! but who can to-cause her sorrows!
(she in beautiful! but who caused her sorrows!)

la pauvre fille, elle aime un ingrat qui la fuit hélas!
the poor girl, she loves an ingrate who her left alas!
(the poor girl, she loves an ingrate: do you know that ingrate?)

la pauvre fille aime un ingrat: cet ingrat, sais-tu?
the poor girl loves an ingrate: that ingrate, know-you?
(the poor girl loves an ingrate: do you know that ingrate?)

c'est toi même, toi qui la conduis au trépas,
it's your self, you who her leads to-the death,
(It's you yourself, who leads her to death,)

oui, toi, toi même; ne detourne pas la vue
yes, you, your self; not turn-away not the view
(yes, you, you yourself; don't turn away your view)

un seul regard par charité, un seul regard!
a single glance for charity, a single glance!
(a single glance of pity, a single glance!)

Vois comme elle est émue, comme son sein est agité,
Look how she is moved, how her breast is agitated,
(Look how she is moved, how her breast is agitated,)

prends sa main, ah! qu'elle est brulante, pauvre enfant,
take her hand, ah! that-she is burning, poor child,
(take her hand, ah! she is burning, poor child,)

prête à défaillir: dans tes bras la voilà tremblante:
close to failing: in your arms her there-is trembling:
(close to failing: she trembles in your arms:)

ah! veux-tu la laisser mourir? pauvre fille,
ah! wish-you her to-let to-die? poor girl,
(ah! do you want her to die? poor girl,)

tu la vois prête à mourir ah! non tu vas l'aimer,
you her see close to dying ah! not you go her-to-love,
(you see her close to dying ah! you don't go to love her,)

viens, viens, viens, ah! tu vas l'aimer, viens, viens.
come, come, come, ah! you go her-to-love, come, come.
(come, come, come, ah! go to love her, come, come.)

(Le novice:) Où suis-je?
(The novice:) Where am-I?
(The novice:) (Where am I)

(Le malin:) Viens!
(The evil:) Come!
(The evil:) (Come!)

(Le novice:) L'enfer!
(The novice:) The-hell!
(The novice:) (Hell!)

(Le malin:) Viens!
(The evil:) Come!
(The evil:) (Come!)

(Le novice:) l'enfer, l'enfer, l'enfer, je meurs d'effroi!
(The novice:) the-hell, the-hell, the-hell, I die of-fear!
(The novice:) (hell, hell, hell, I am dying of fear!)

D'où viennent ces accents?
Of-where come these words?
(Where do these words come from?)

est-ce encore un prestige sauvez-moi, mon Dieu, sauvez-moi!
is that again an illusion save-me, my God, save-me!
(is that an allusion again, save me, my God, save me!)

Mais non, j'entends sonner l'heure de la prière,
But no, I-hear sounding the-hour of the prayer,
(But no, I hear the hour of prayer sounding,)

voici venir le moment solennel;
here comes the moment solemn;
(here comes the solemn moment;)

je vais entrer au divin sanctuaire,
I go to-enter to-the divine sanctuary,
(I go to enter the divine sanctuary.)

je vais goûter les delices du ciel.
I go to-taste the delights of-the heaven.
(I go to taste the delights of heaven.)

Ces plaisir, ces époux, cette femme,
Those pleasures, those spouses, that girl,
(Those pleasures, that couple, that girl,)

l'enfer: non, non, non, non, c'est un songe,
the-hell: no, no, no, no, it's a dream,
(hell: no, no, no, no, its a dream,)

un vain songe: je vais enfin entrer au divin sanctuaire;
a vain dream: I go at-last to-enter to-the divine sanctuary;
(a vain dream: I'm finally going to enter the divine sanctuary;)

je vais goûter les délices du ciel.
I go to-taste the delights of-the heaven.
(I go to taste the delights of heaven.)

O mon ange, je vais goûter enfin les délices du ciel.
Oh my angel, I go to-taste at-last the delights of-the heaven.
(Oh my angel, at last I go to taste the delights of heaven.)

(See Donizetti - L'ultima notte di un novizio)

La lontananza
The distance

Or ch'io sono a te rapita,
Now that-I am to you enraptured,
(Now that I am enraputred with you,)

or che tolto a me
now that taken from me
(now that you have taken)

tu sei colle spine di mia vita
you have with-the sorrows of my life
(from me the sorrows of my life,)

gli altrui fior non cangerei,
the other flowers not change,
(the other flowers do not change,)

se a soffrir e solo un core,
if to suffer is alone a heart,
(if a heart alone is to suffer,)

quel soffrir si fa dolore,
that to-suffer so makes pain,
(that suffering makes so much pain,)

caro amor. Ah! caro amor!
dear love. Ah! dear love!
(dear love. Ah! dear love!)

Donizetti
La mère et l'enfant
The mother and the-infant

Un voile blanc couvrait la terre,
A veil white covered the earth,
(A white veil covered the earth,)

la neige en gros flocons tombait:
the snow in large flakes fell:
(in large flakes snow fell:)

et retenu dans sa carriere captif le torrent s'arrêtait;
and retained in its course captive the torrent it-stopped;
(and held in its course captive the stopped torrent;)

l'hiver partant désolait la nature;
the-winter leaving desolated the nature;
(winter left nature desolated;)

on dit qu'alors dans sa mansarde obscure, une mère pleurait,
it says that-then in its garret dark, a mother cried,
(then in a dark garret a mother cried,)

et la mort dans le sein, disait:
and the death in the breast, said:
(and with death in her breast said:)

du pain, du pain, oh! s'il vous plait,
of-the bread, of-the bread, oh! if-it you please,
(some bread, some bread, oh! please, some bread!

du pain! mon pauvre enfant se meurt de faim.
of-the bread! my poor infant he dies of hunger.
(my poor baby is dying of hunger.)

Pour t'epargner des maux horribles
For him-to-save from-the harms horrible
(I have spared nothing in this world)

rien au monde ne m'a coûté:
nothing in-the world not me-has spared:
(to save him from horrible harm:)

le travail, les veilles pénibles ont hélas! détruit ma santé.
the work, the vigils painful have alas! destroyed my health.
(work, painful vigils alas! have destroyed my health.)

L'âme brisée et voyant ta souffrance,
The-soul broken and seeing your suffering,
(With broken spirit and seeing your suffering,)

j'ai des passans mendié l'assistance,
I-have of-the passers-by begged the-assistance,
(I have begged for help from some passers-by,)

oui, pour toi, mon enfant, oui, j'ai tendu la main,
yes, for you, my infant, yes, I-have held the hand,
(yes, for you, my baby, yes, I have begged,)

disant: du pain, du pain, oh! s'il vous plait....
saying: of-the bread, of-the bread, oh! if-it you please....
(saying: some bread, some bread, ah! please....)

Ici personne pour m'entendre!
Here no-one to me-hears!
(Here no one hears me!)

mes cris, mes maux sont superflus:
my cries, my hardships are superfluous:
(my cries, my hardships are superfluous:)

ah! jusqu'à demain, s'il faut attendre, ni lui,
ah! until tomorrow, if-it makes to-wait, neither him,
(ah! until tomorrow, if it waits that long, neither him,)

ni moi ne serons plus; du pain....
nor me not will-be more, of the bread....
(nor me will be any more, some bread....)

Donizetti
La ninna nanna
The Lullaby

Dormi, fanciullo mio, dormi e riposa nella pace del sonno
Sleep, son my, sleep and rest in-the peace of-the sleep
(Sleep, my son, sleep and rest in the peace of transparent)

trasparente, dormi, sì, dormi, e la pupilla ascosa
transparent, sleep, yes, sleep, and the pupil hidden
(sleep, sleep, yes, sleep, and the hidden eye will silently)

si volga al ciel silenziosamente.
itself turns to-the sky silently.
(turn itself toward the sky.)

Dormi, dormi, i Cherubini a te scherzano
Sleep, sleep, the Cherubs to you they-play
(Sleep, sleep, the Cherubs play)

d'accanto; i lor labbri porporini stanno aperti a dolce canto.
beside-you; the their lips purple are open to sweet song.
(beside you; their purple lips are open to the sweet song.)

Uno spirto t'han creduto dalle sfere qui caduto
A spirit you-they-have believed from-the spheres here fallen
(They believe that you are a spirit fallen here from the spheres)

ed al coro a cui tu manchi ricondurti
and to-the heart to which you are-missing
(and want to take you back to the sky)

vonno in ciel,
to-take-you-back they-want in sky,
(to the heart which misses you,)

figlio mio, ricondurti vonno in ciel.
son my, to-take-you-back they-want in sky.
(oh my son, they want to take you back into the sky.)

Ah! dormi, dormi, o figlio mio, ah!
Ah! sleep, sleep, oh son my, ah!
(Ah! sleep, sleep, my son, ah!)

dormi il sonno della pace, figlio mio, dormi,
sleep the sleep of-the peace, son my, sleep,
(sleep the sleep of peace, my son, sleep,)

dormi, gli occhi stanchi covra il sonno col suo vel,
sleep, the eyes tired cover the sleep with-the its veil,
(sleep, your tired eyes sleep covers with its veil,)

ah! dormi, dormi, ah! Ah! dormi.
ah! sleep, sleep, ah! Ah! sleep.
(ah! sleep, sleep, ah! Ah! sleep.)

Ah! sì, non senti un'alito
Ah! yes, not you-hear a breath
(Ah! yes, don't you hear a breath)

che ti carezza il viso? Ah! sì, non vedi gli angioli
which you caresses the face? Ah! yes, not you-see the angels
(which caresses your face? Ah! yes, don't you see the angels)

scesi dal paradiso che intorno
descended from-the paradise that around
(descended from paradise that surround you)

a te s'aggirano come farfalle ai fior,
to you they-encircle like butterflies to-the flowers,
(like butterflies around flowers, don't you see the angels,)

non vedi gli angioli, o figlio mio....
not you-see the angels, o son my....
(o my son....)

E la tua culla argentea
And the your cradle silvery
(And your silvery cradle)

come una navicella solca tranquilla l'etere,
as a little-ship plows quiet the-ether,
as a little ship plows the ether quietly,)

Passa di stella in stella, vogano lieti gli angioli,
Passes from star to star, they-row happy the angels,
(It passes from star to star, the angels happily row,)

tu dormi in mezzo a lor,
you sleep in among of them,
(you sleep in among them,)

in mezzo a gli angioli, o figlio mio,
in among to the angels, o son my,
(in among the angels, o my son,)

tu dormi in mezzo agli angioli, o figlio, o figlio mio....
you sleep in among to-the angels, oh son, oh son my....
(you sleep in among the angels, oh son, oh my son....)

La Sultana
The Sultana

Là sedeva, sull'erto verone,
There she-did-sit, on-the-rising balcony,
(There she sat, on her high balcony,)

in un'estasi muta d'amore;
in an-ecstasy muted of-love;
(in a love-muted ecstasy;)

d'un destriero al nitrito,
of-a steed to-the neigh,
(like a steed in a neigh,)

il suo core d'un insolita gioia brillò.
the your heart of-an unusual joy I-will-sparkle.
(I will sparkle in your heart with an unusual joy.)

E la notte col manto stellato,
And the night with-the mantle starry,
(And the night with its starry mantle,)

d'un sorriso allegrava il creato,
of-a smile happy the creation,
(the creation with a happy smile,)

e dal colle lontano, s'udia un tenero canto d'amor.
and of-the hills far-away, they-hear a tender song of-love.
(and the hills far away, hear a tender song of love,)

"Bello è il cielo cogl'astri dorati,
"Beautiful is the heaven with-the-stars adorned,
("Beautiful is the heaven with its adorned stars,)

è soave ogni raggio di stella,
is sweet every ray of star,
(every ray of the star is sweet,)

ma del cielo degl'astri più bella è colei
but of-the heaven of-the-stars more beautiful is with-her
(but the heaven of the stars is more beautiful with her)

che m'impera sul cor, è più bella del sole,
that me-she-ruled on-the heart, is more beautiful of-the sun,
(now that she rules on my heart, the sun is more beautiful,)

più bella del ciel."
more beautiful of-the heaven."
(the heaven is more beautiful.")

Fuggi, o caro, sclamava la mesta,
Flee, o dear-one, she-did-exclaim the sadness,
(Flee, o dear one, the sadness she exclaimed,)

va t'invola al mio truce tiranno;
go you-steal to-the my cruel tyrant;
(go steal away to my cruel tyrant;)

già il pugnale egli aguzza in tuo danno
already the dagger he sharpens in your harm
(already he sharpens his dagger to harm you)

sua vendetta sul capo ti stà, si ti stà.
its vendetta on-the head your rests, yes your rests.
(its vendetta on your head rests, yes on yours rests.)

Sì sclamava e la luna fratanto del suo volto
Thus it-exclaimed and the moon meanwhile of-the your face)
(Thus it exclaimed and meanwhile the moon on your face)

velava l'incanto e dal colle lontano s'udia
rose the-enchantment and of-the hills far-away they-hear
(rose the enchantment and the hills far away hear)

un tenero canto d'amor.   Passò un giorno,
a tender song of-love.   I-will-pass a day,
(a tender song of love.   I will pass the day,)

la notte riedea, il destriero nitriva, ma invano;
the night did-laugh, the steed did-neigh, but in vain;
(the night did laugh, the steed did neigh, but in vain;)

la Sultana al veron non siedea,
the Sultana to-the balcony not she-did-sit,
(the Sultana did not sit on the balcony,)

caldo sangue macchiava il veron.
hot blood it-did-stain the balcony.
(hot blood did stain the balcony.)

Pur la notte col manto stellato d'un sorriso allegrava
Now the night with-the mantle starry of-a smile happy
(Now the night with its starry mantle, the creation)

il creato e dal colle lontano, lontano,
the creation and of-the hills far-away, far-away,
(with a happy smile and on the hills far away, far away,)

s'udia il tenero canto d'amor.
they-hear the tender song of-love.
(they hear the tender song of love.)

Donizetti
La Zingara
The gypsy

La zingara. La zingara.
The gypsy. The gypsy.
(The gypsy. The gypsy.)

Fra l'erbe cosparse di rorido gelo,
Among the-grass sprinkled with dewey frost,
(Among the dewey frosted grass,)

coverta del solo gran manto del cielo,
covered by-the only large mantle of-the sky,
(covered only by the large dark sky,)

mia madre esultando la vita mi diè.
my mother rejoicing the life to-me gave.
(my rejoicing mother gave birth to me.)

Fanciulla, sui greppi le capre emulai;
Young-girl, on-the cliffs the goats I-emulated;
(As a young girl, I emulated the goats on the cliffs;)

per ville e cittadi, cresciuta, danzai,
through villages and towns, growing-up, I-danced,
(growing up I danced through villages and towns,)

le dame lor palme distesero a me.
the ladies their palms extended to me.
(the ladies extended their palms to me.)

La ra la ah la zingara.
La ra la ah the gypsy.
(La ra la ah the gypsy.)

Io loro predissi le cose non notte,
I to-them would-predict the things not noticable,
(I would predict unknown things to them,)

ne feci dolenti, ne feci beate,
some I-made sad, some I-made happy,
(I made some sad, I made some happy,)

segreti conobbi di sdegno, d'amor.
secrets I-knew of disdain, of-love.
(I knew secrets of disdain, of love.)

La ra la ah la zingara.
La ra la ah the gypsy.
(La ra la ah the gypsy.)

Un giorno la mano mi porte un donzello;
One day the hand to-me brought a page;
(One day a page brought me his hand;)

mai visto non fummi garsone più bello;
never seen any handsome boy more beautiful;
(I had never seen a more handsome boy;)

oh! s'ei nella destra leggessemi il cor!
oh! if-he in-the right-hand would-read to-me the heart!
(oh! if he would read my heart in my right hand!)

La zingara, ah, la zingara, si!
The gypsy, ah, the gypsy, yes!
(The gypsy, ah, the gypsy, yes!)

Donizetti
Le Crèpuscule
The twilight

L'aube naît et ta porte est close:
The-dawn rises and its door is closed:
(The dawn rises and its door is closed:)

oh ma belle, pourquoi sommeiler?
oh my beautiful-one, why do-you-sleep?
(oh my beautiful one, why do you sleep?)

A l'heure où s'eveille la rose
At the-hour where itself-wakes the rose
(At the hour when the rose awakes)

ne vas-tu pas te réveiller?
not go-you not to-wake?
(you do not awake?)

Oh, ma charmante,
Oh, my charming-one,
(Oh my charming one,)

écoute ici l'amant qui chante et pleure aussi.
listen here the-lover who sings and cries also.
(listen here to the lover who sings and cries also.)

Tout frappe à ta porte bénie,
All knock at your door blessed,
(Everyone knocks at your blessed door,)

l'aurore dit: je suis le jour;
the-morning says: I am the day;
(the morning says: I am day;)

l'oiseau dit: je suis l'harmonie; et mon coeur dit:
the-bird says: I am the-harmony; and my heart says:
(the bird says: I am harmony; and my heart says:)

je suis l'amour. Je t'adore ange, je t'aime, femme,
I am the-love. I you-adore angel, I you-love, woman,
(I am love. I adore you angel, I love you, wife,)

Dieu qui pour toi m'a complété
God who for you me-has completed
(God who for you has completed)

a fait mon amour pour ton âme
to make my love for your soul
(me by making my love for your soul)

et mon regard, pour ta beauté, oh, ma charmante....
and my gaze, for your beauty, oh, my charming-one....
(and my gaze, for your beauty, oh, my charming one....)

Donizetti
L'ultima notte di un novizio
The-last night of a novice

(Il novizio:) (The novice:)

Doman, quando la squilla annunzi la preghiera,
Tomorrow, when the chime announces the prayer,
(Tomorrow, when the prayer bell rings,)

mi prostrerò devoto al sacro altar.
me I-will-prostrate devoted to-the sacred altar.
(I will devoutly prostrate myself at the sacred altar.)

Verrà dal ciel su me la luce;
It-will-come from-the heaven on me the light;
(Light will come from the heaven onto me;)

d'un sacro nodo l'alma a innebriar.
of-a sacred bond the-soul to inebriate.
(to inebriate my soul with a sacred bond.)

Fino a domani l'indugio ancora,
Until to tomorrow the-delay still,
(There is still a delay until tomorrow,)

oh! notte lenta, affretta il piè; si, si, t'affretta,
oh! night slow, hasten the foot; yes, yes, you-hasten,
(oh! slow night, hasten your foot; yes, yes, hasten yourself,)

rechi l'aurora il più bel giorno
you-bring the-daybreak the most beautiful day
(bring the daybreak to the most beautiful day)

che splenda a me.
that shines on me.
(that shines on me.)

E tu in me scendi, divino spirto, scendi e favellami
And you in me shine, divine spirit, shine and speak-to-me
(And shine in me, divine spirit, shine and speak to me)

nel mio sopor di quella pace ond'io deliro,
in-the my drowsiness of that peace of-which-I rave,
(of that peace which I dream about in my sleep,)

che verrà col nuovo albor.
that it-will-come with-the new dawn.
(that it will come with the new dawn.)

(Lo spirito maligno:) (The spirit evil:)

Una speranza menzognera i tuoi sensi pretende ingannar.
A hope false the your senses pretent to-deceive.
(A false hope pretends to deceive your senses.)

Che? diviso dal mondo,
What? divided from-the world,
(What? seperated from the world,)

tra il chiostro e la preghiera,
among the cloister and the prayer,
(among cloister and prayer,)

speri tu la pace trovar?
hope you the peace to-find?
(you hope to find peace?)

Ah! non provasti ancor le gioie della vita, ah,
Ah! not tried still the joys of-the life, ah,
(Ah! you still haven't tried the joys of life, ah,)

tu non provasti l'estasi che può rapire un cor.
you not to-try-you the-ecstasy that can to-ravish a heart.
(you didn't try the ecstasy that can ravish a heart.)

Dio ti volea felice, tutto a goder t'invita,
God you wanted happy, all to enjoy you-he-invites,
(God wanted you to be happy, he invites you to enjoy
everything,)

tu sprezzeresti, ingrato,
you would-scorn-yourself, ingrate,
(you would-scorn-yourself, ingrate,)

il don del tuo fattor?
the gift of-the your maker?
(the gift of your maker?)

T'arresta, è tempo ancor; seguimi e sii felice, vieni!
You-it-stops, is time still; follow-me and be happy, come!
(Time stops you, there is still time; follow me and be happy,
come!)

(Il novizio:) (The novice:)

Che intesi mai? chi mai mi tragge a sè?
What I-understand indeed? who never me it-draws to itself?
(What do I hear? who draws me to himself?)

No, non fu che un sogno...o Vergin protettrice, proteggimi,
No, not was that a dream...o Virgin protectress, protect-me,
(No, that was nothing but a dream...o Virgin protectress,
protect me,)

proteggimi, no, no, non ti scordar di me,
protect-me, no, no, not you to-forget of me,
(protect me, no, no, don't forget me,)

no, fino al novello albor.
no, until to-the first dawn.
(no, before the break of dawn.)

Ave Maria, gratia plena, Dominus tecum benedicta.
Hail Mary, grace full, God you-with blessed.
(Hail Mary, full of grace, may blessed God be with you.)

(Lo spirito maligno:) (The spirit evil:)

Guarda colà, di che caldo amor s'aman
Look over-there, of what hot love themselves-loving
(Look over there, what warm love between themselves)

fra lor quei novelli sposi, mira gli sguardi,
among their those new spouses, observe the glances,
(has that new couple, watch their glances,)

odi l'ascoso ardor stemprarsi in sospiri amorosi,
hear the-secret ardor melts-it in sighs loving,
(hear the secret ardor melting itself in loving sighs,)

e quel bambin che d'angelo divin tutti ha gl'incanti,
and that baby who from-angel divine all it-has the-charms,
(and that baby has all the charms of a divine angel,)

e il dolce sorriso per lui l'ardor
and the sweet smile for him the-ardor
(and the sweet smile for him has doubled the ardor)

s'addoppia dell'amor,
itself-doubled of-the-love,
(of their love,)

sì, sì, per lui, e la terra si cangia in paradiso.
yes, yes, for him, and the earth itself changes into paradise.
(yes, yes, for him, and the earth itself has changed into
paradise.)

Oh, qual gioir!
Oh, what joy!
(Oh, what a delight!)

Perchè tu il vuoi fuggir? vieni a bear, deh! vieni.
Why you it wish to-flee? come to be-happy, ah! come.
(Why do you wish to flee? come and be happy, ah! come.)

(Il novizio:) (The novice:)

Ah! pietà di me, ah! Ciel, pietà, o Vergin, pietà!
Ah! pity of me, ah! Heaven, pity, oh Virgin, pity!
(Ah! have pity on me, ah! Heaven, have pity, oh Virgin, have
pity!)

Ma io sognai, sognai sol per te,
But I dreamed, I-dreamed only for you,
(But I have dreamed, I have dreamed only for you,)

Vergin pia, sol per te mi destai, pietà,
Virgin pious, only for you me I-awoke, pity,
(pious Virgin, only for you have I awoken, have pity,)

Vergin pia, m'assisti
Virgin pious, me-you-assist
(pious Virgin, assist me)

Io fido in te, o Vergin protettrice,
I believe in you, o Virgin protectress,
(I believe in you, oh Virgin protectress,)

non ti scostar da me.
not you move-away from me.
(don't move away from me.)

Ave Maria, gratia plena, Dominus tecum benedicta....
Hail Mary, grace full, God you-with blessed....
(Hail Mary, full of grace, may blessed God be with you....)

(Lo spirito maligno:) (The spirit evil:)

Oh! dove muove quella donzella?
Oh! where moves that young-girl?
(Oh! where does that young girl go?)

coperta il volto d'atro pallor?
hidden the face of-horrible pallor?
(with her face of horrible pallor hidden?)

in sua mestizia ancora è bella!
in her sadness still is beautiful!
(even in her sadness she is beautiful!)

quale ha nel seno cagion di dolor? ahi! trista ancora,
what she-has in-the breast reason of sorrow? ah! sad still,
(what reason for sorrow has she in her breast? ah! still sad,)

sì, t'ama,
yes, you-she-loves,
(yes, she loves you,)

e tu hai cor di lasciarla partir?
and you have heart of to-allow-her to-leave?
(and you have the heart to allow her to leave?)

la vedi là.
her you-see there.
(you see her there.)

Ah! non torcer le pupille la quarda almen,
Ah! not to-turn the eyes her glance at-least,
(Ah! don't you at least turn your eyes to look,)

per pietà ah! La mira, vedi, geme e sospira,
for pity ah! Her you-see, look, she-moans and she-sighs,
(For pity's sake, ah! You see her, look, she moans and sighs,)

se non l'aiti, ella morrà;
if not her-you-help, she will-die;
(if you don't help her, she will die;)

l'amante stringi, senti,
the-lover you-hold, you-feel,
(the lover holds you, you feel,)

le manca sino il respir sul tuo seno
to-her lacks even it to-breath on-the your breast
(she fails even you hold her breath already breathing)

è già spirante: ah! la man le stringi,
is already breathing: ah! the hand of-her you-hold,
(on your breast: ah! you hold her hand,)

si, ah! vuoi tu vederla morir?
yes, ah! wish you to-see-her to-die?
(yes, ah! do you wish to see her die?)

Ah! no, tu l'ami ancor,
Ah! no, you her-love still,
(Ah! no, you still love her,)

vieni tocca, ah! sì, tu l'ami ancor, sì, sì!
come her-touch, ah! yes, you her-love still, yes, yes!
(come touch her, ah! yes, you still love her, yes, yes!)

(Il novizio:) Ove sono? (Il spirito) Vieni!
(The novice:) Where I-am? (The spirit:) Come!
(The novice:) (Where am I?) (The spirit:) (Come!)

(Il novizio:) L'inferno! (Lo spirito:) Vieni!
(The novice:) The-inferno! (The spirit:) Come!
(The novice:) (Hell!) (The spirit:) (Come!)

(Il novizio:) (The novice:)

L'inferno, ohimè, ohimè, m'opprime il terror!
The-inferno, alas, alas, me-it-oppresses the terror!
(Hell, alas, alas, terror oppresses me!)

Ma quale rimbomba, qual flebile suono, ah! di me, pietà,
But what booms, what mournful sound, ah! of me, pity,
(But what roars, what mournful sound, ah! on me have pity,)

Signor, pietà!
Lord, pity!
(Lord, have pity!)

Ma no, squillar già s'ode l'ora della preghiera
But no, ringing already itself-hears the-hour of-the prayer
(But no, I hear the prayer bell ringing already)

già m'attende il sacro altar;
already me-awaits the sacred altar;
(the sacred altar awaits me;)

entrar potrò nella diletta schiera,
to-enter I-will-be-able-to in-the delight group,
(I will-be-able-to enter into the group of delight,)

il cielo alfine arride al mio pregar.
the heaven at-last smiles to-the my prayer.
(heaven at last smiles on my prayer.)

Quell'amor, quel bambin, quella donzella l'inferno, no, no,
That-love, that baby, that young-girl the-inferno, no, no,
(That love, that baby, that young girl, hell, no, no,)

Vergin pia, tu m'assisti affido
Virgin pious, you me-assist I-entrust
(pious Virgin, assist me, in you I trust)

in te entrar potrò, si, si.
in you to-enter I-will-be-able-to, yes, yes.
(that I will-be-able-to enter, yes, yes.)

La Vergin pia, alfine arride al mio pregar.
The Virgin pious, at-last smiles to-the my prayer.
(The pious Virgin, at last smiles on my prayer.)

(See Donizetti - La dernière nuit d'un novice)

Donizetti
Lu trademiento
The betrayal

Ah! tradetore, tu m'haje lassata
Ah! traitor, you me-have left
(Ah! traitor, you have left me)

e m'haje scagnata pe chella llà,
and me-you-have exchanged for that-one there,
(and you have exchanged me for that one there,)

gnorsì, che chella de me è chiù bella, gnorsì,
yes-sir, because that-one of me is more beautiful, yes-sir,
(yes sir, because that one is more beautiful than me, yes sir,)

ma pe fedele po se vedrà.
but for fidelity then one will-see.
(but then for fidelity one will see.)

Lu trademiento ca mo me
The betrayal that now to-me
(The betrayal that now you do)

faje non passa craje, te lo farà.
you-do not pass away, to-you it she-will-do.
(to me doesn't go away, she will do it to you.)

E cheste lagreme che mo m'annozzano, gnorsì,
Are these tears which now me-choke, yes-sir,
(These are tears which now choke me, yes sir,)

porzi co ausura l'haje da scunttà.
bring with usury it-you-have of to-pay-for.
(as brings with usury you have to pay for it.)

Meine Liebe
My Love

Ja, ich lieb' doch meine Liebe, keines Menschen Herz
Yes, I love indeed my beloved, no man's heart
(Yes, I indeed love my beloved, no man's heart)

schliesst ein: Gott nur kennet diese Triebe,
includes it: God alone knows these desires,
(encompasses it: only God knows these desires,)

hier auf Erden ich nur allein.
here on earth I only alone.
(here on earth only I alone do know.)

Wohnet in der Seele Heiligthume, gleich dem Dufte,
Dwells in the soul's sanctuary, like the aroma,
(Though she dwells in the soul's sanctuary, like the aroma,)

der im dem Kelch der Blume, dort verborgen stille ruht,
which in the cup of-the flower, there hidden silently rests,
(which in the flower's cup, there rests silently hidden,)

Bei Gelag und munterm Sange,
By merrymaking and lively singing,
(By merrymaking and lively singing,)

in der Jugend Reih'n und Fraum,
in of youth's rows and exhuberance,
(in youth's company and exhuberance,)

wohnt sie nicht, denn bei solchem Klange,
dwells she not, for near such sound,
(she does not dwell, for near such sound,)

ist für sie nicht Ort und Raum,
is for her no place and space,
(there is no place or space for her,)

denn sie ist von reinster Seele,
for she is of-the purest soul,
(for her soul is the purest,)

ist ein Bildniss sonder Fehler,
is an image without blemish,
(is an image without blemish)

ist der Tugend Blüth' und Glanz.
is of virtue's blossom and sparkle.
(is of virtue's blossom and sparkle.)

Wo sie weile, und wie ihr Name, ist Geheimnis,
Where she dwells, and what her name, is secret,
(Where she dwells, and what her name is, is secret,)

ja selbst für mich, mir im Herzen, spriesset ihr Same
yes even for me, to-me in-my heart, sprouts her seed
(yes even for me, in my heart, sprouts her seed)

doch sie selber erfasste ich nicht.
yet she herself grasp I not.
(yet she herself I do not grasp.)

Hier in diesen finstern Erdenreichen,
Here in these dark earthly-realms,
(Here is these dark earthly realms,)

giebt kein Bild es, das ihr könnte gleichen, nur das Herz
There no picture is, that her could equal, only the heart
(gives no picture, that could equal her, only the heart)

vermag es ferne zu schau'n. Ah! vermag es ferne zu schau'n.
can it from-afar to view. Ah! can it from-afar to view.
(can view it from afar. Ah! can view it from afar.)

(See Donizetti - L'amor mio)

Me voglio fa 'na casa
For-me I-want to-build a house

Me voglio fa 'na casa miezo mare
For-me I-want to-build a house in-the-middle sea
(I want to build a house for myself in the middle of the sea)

fravecata de penne de pavune tralla la le tra la la
fabricated of feathers of peacocks tralla la le tra la la
(made of peacock feathers tralla, la le tra la la)

d'oro e d'argiento li scaline fare e de prete preziuse
of-gold and of-silver the steps to-make and of stones precious
(the steps of gold and silver, and the balcony)

li barcune tralla la le la.
the balcony tralla la le la.
(of precious stones tralla la le la.)

Quanno Nannella mia se va a facciare ognuno dice
When Little-girl my herself goes to appear everyone says
(When my Nannella goes to show herself everyone says)

mo sponta lu sole....
now rises the sun....
(now the sun rises....)

Donizetti
"Nè ornerà la bruna chioma"
"Of-it will-adorn the brown head-of-hair"

Maggior di nostra speme oggi campagne
Bigger of our hopes today countrysides
(Larger than our hopes of today great quantities)

disperdan le selve, a' patrii tetti parte
to-disperse the great-quantities, to-the native houses divide
(disperse into the countrysides, divide to the native houses)

sen rechi e se ne serbi parte
they-feel you-bring and if of-it reserves divide
(as you wish, and the reserves divide)

in dono agli stranieri.
in gift to-the foreigners.
(as gifts to the foreigners.)

Ampio da lor riporterem tesoro
Ample of them we-will-bring-back treasure
(Abundant of them we will bring back)

delle dovizie che al possente duce
of-the wealth that to-the powerful leader
(wealth of the powerful leader)

il lontano da noi mondi produce.
the far from us worlds productive.
(from the far away productive worlds.)

Nè ornerà la bruna chioma qualche gemma rilucente,
Of-it will-adorn the brown head-of-hair some gem shining,
(Some gem from it will adorn the brown head of hair,)

che a guerrieri dell'Oriente
that to warriors of-the-Orient
(that to Oriental warriors)

più bel sol pingendo va.
more beautiful alone pushing go.
(more beautiful alone trudgingly go.)

E la figlia del deserto, abbellita da quel serto,
And the daughter of-the desert, adorned of that wreath,
(And the daughter of the desert, adorned with that wreath,)

qualche grazia agl'occhio loro, qualche vezzo acquisterà.
some grace to-the-eyes their, some necklace will-obtain.
(with grace to their eyes, will obtain some necklaces.)

Caro bene, al tuo cospetto vani fregi io non desio.
Dear beloved, to-the your sight vainly you-adorn I not desire.
(Dear beloved, I do not desire your vainly adorned sight.)

Bella sol dell'amor mio, nel tuo seno volerò.
Beautiful sun of-the-love my, in-the your breast I-will-fly.
(Beautiful sun of my love, I will fly to your breast.)

Se tu m'ami o mio diletto, ogni bella io vincerò.
If you me-loved oh my delight, every beautiful I will-win.
(If you loved me, oh my delight, I will win everything
beautiful.)

Donizetti
Ov'e la voce magica...
Where-is the voice magic...

Ov'è la voce magica le magiche parole
Where-is the voice magic the magic words
(Where is the magic voice, the magic words)

della leggiadra vergine più
of-the graceful virgin more
(of the graceful virgin who is more)

cara a me del sole?
dear to me of-the sun?
(dear to me than the sun?)

Perché non più quell'alito che innebria,
Why not more that-breath that inebriates,
(Why no more that breath which inebriates,)

che innamora?
that fills-with-love?
(that fills with love?)

Oh! La sua voce ancora che mi parlò d'amor!
Oh! The her voice still that me it-spoke of-love!
(Oh! That voice which still spoke to me of love!)

Ch'io l'oda, o ciel tal grazia
That-I her-hear, oh heaven so-much grace
(That I might hear her, oh heaven do not deny me)

negata a me non sia;
denied to me not be;
(so much grace;)

ogni mio bene toglimi ogni speranza mia,
every my beloved taken-from-me every hope my,
(my beloved has taken from me every hope,)

e in quel supremo gaudio s'egl'è destin ch'io morrà,
and in that last joy if-he-is destined that-I will-die,
(if he is destined that I will die, in that last joy,)

a quella voce allora io mirirò d'amor.
to that voice then I will-die of-love.
(then to that voice I will die of love.)

Donizetti
Romanza moresca
Moorish romance

Il mio grido io getto ai venti perché il portin da qui
The my cry I throw to-the winds because the door of here
(I throw my cry to the winds because she never comes)

lunge ed il suon de miei lamenti fino
long and the sound of my laments until
(to this door to my long)

ad ella mai non giunge.
to she never not comes.
(and lamenting sounds.)

O pastore, hai tu veduta la mia donna ch'ho perduta?
O shepherd, have you seen the my woman that-I-have lost?
(O shepherd, have you seen my woman whom I have lost?)

L'hai tu veduta? I suoi sgardi son due freccie,
She-have you seen? The her glances are two arrows,
(Have you seen her? Her face has two piercing eyes,)

come il giglio ha bianco il viso,
as the lily she-has white the face,
(her face is white as a lily,)

come il corvo ha nere trece,
as the raven she-has black tresses,
(her black tresses like a raven,)

come l'alba ha dolce il riso;
like the-dawn she-has sweet the smile;
(she has a sweet smile like the dawn;)

e si chiama Juanita/Caterina.
and one calls Juanita/Caterina.
(and she is called Juanita/Caterina.)

La mia donna ch'è fuggirà.
The my woman that-is flown.
(My woman has fled.)

Son tre giorni e son tre notti
Are three days and are three nights
(It has been three days and three nights)

che la cerco e non la trovo;
that her I-seek and not her I find;
(since I have sought and not found her;)

per dirupi aspri e dirotti i miei passi incarno io muovo.
for crags rough and weeping the my steps I-would I move.
(through rough crags and bitter weeping my steps moved.)

Dimmi, hai tu veduta la mia donna
Tell-me, have you seen the my woman
(Tell me, have you seen my woman)

ch'io perduta?
that-I lost?
(whom I have lost?)

Donizetti
Sovra il campo della vita
On the field of-the life

Sovra il campo della vita sono pianta abbandonata.
On the field of-the life I-am crying abandoned.
(On the field of life I am crying abandoned.)

La misura ho già stancata dell'immenso mio dolor.
The misery I-have already tired of-the-immense my sorrow.
(I have already tired of the misery of my immense sorrow.)

Senza nome, senza patria erro ignota a tutte genti.
Without name, without fatherland I-was unknown to all men.
(Without name, without fatherland I was unknown to all men.)

Cerco un eco a miei lamenti;
I-search an echo to my laments;
(I search an echo to my laments;)

sol lo trovo in mezzo al cor.
alone it I-find in center to-the heart.
(alone I find it in the center of my heart.)

Su l'onda tremola
On the-wave trembling

Su l'onda tremola, ride la luna,
On the-wave trembling, laughs the moon,
(On the trembling wave, the moon laughs,)

regna il silenzio sulla laguna.
reigns the silence on-the lagoon.
(silence reigns on the lagoon.)

Bice, t'aspetta la mia barchetta,
Bice, you-it-waits the my little-boat,
(Bice, my little boat awaits you,)

ma perché palpiti? di che temer?
but why you-palpitate? of who to-tremble?
(but why do you palpitate? of whom do you tremble?)

Ci saprà reggere da Gondoliere questo naviglio
Here it-will-be to-support for Gondolier this canal
(Here you will support this canal for the Gondolier)

di Cipria il figlio, vieni, già l'anima gioia m'inonda,
for Cipria the son, come, already the-soul happy me-floods,
(for his son Cipria, come, already my soul is flooded with
happiness,)

vieni, non vo' più riedere.
come, not I-wish more to-return.
(come, I do not wish to return.)

Bice, alla sponda non voglio un trono,
Bice, to-the bank not I-wish a throne,
(Bice, on the bank I do not want a throne,)

se teco io sono non vo' più riedere...vieni,
if you-with I am not I-wish more to-return...come,
(if I am not with you, I do not wish to return...come,)

io dimentico sul mar tra i venti,
I forget on-the sea among the winds,
(I forget on the wind filled sea,)

che i soavissimi tuoi giuramenti sono più instabili
that the very-gentle your promises are more unstable
(that your very gentle promises are more unstable)

di vento e mar....
of wind and sea....
(than the wind and sea....)

Una lacrima (Preghiera)
A tear (Prayer)

Dio, Dio! che col cenno moderi l'ira
God, God! who with-the sign you-restrain the-ire
(God, God! who, with a sign restrains the ire)

d'un mar che freme Dio! che col cenno
of-a sea that trembles God! that with-the sign
(of a sea that trembles, God! that with a sign)

agli uomini porgi costanza e speme,
to-the men you-pour constancy and hopes,
(you pour constancy and hopes to men,)

stendi la man benefica, sul lungo mio dolor.
you-extend the hand benificent, on-the lasting my sorrow.
(you extend your benificent hand, on my lasting sorrow.)

Non chieggo a te la tenera gioja del cor felice
Not I-ask to you the tender joy of-the heart happy
(Not do I ask you for the tender joy of a happy heart)

non la speranza provvida d'affanno incantatrice,
not the hope provident of-excitement enchantress,
(nor the provident hope of the enchantress of excitement,)

ti chieggo sol la lagrima, che scioglie il gelo al cor, Ah!
you I-ask only the tear, that melts the cold to-the heart, Ah!
(I ask you only for the tear, that melts the cold of the heart,
Ah!)

Puccini
A Te
To You

Ho! quant'io t'amo, O quanto in me forte è il desio,
Oh! how-I you-love, O how in me strong is the desire,
(Oh! how I love you, O how strong is the desire in me,)

Di stringerti al cuor mio, Di farti palpitar.
To hold-you to-the heart my, To make-you to-palpitate.
(To hold you in my heart, To make you palpitate.)

Da te così lontano Io sòffro, io sòffro assai;
From you thus far-away I suffer, I suffer so-much;
(I suffer so far away from you, I suffer so much;)

Né pace io trovo mai Perchè troppo è l'amore,
Nor peace I find never Because too-much is the-love,
(Nor do I find peace Because love is too strong,)

Troppo è l'amor!
Too-much is the-love!
(Love is too strong!)

O mia vittoria, O mio tesoro,
O my victory, O my treasure,
(O my victory, O my treasure,)

O bene mio, O mio sol pensiero,
O beloved my, O my only thought,
(O my beloved, O my only thought,)

E dammi un bacio e il mondo intiero,
And give-me a kiss and the world entire,
(And give me a kiss and the entire world,)

E mi farai tutto obbliar.
And me will-make all to-forget.
(And it will make me forget everything.)

O mia vittoria, O mio tesor sarà, O bene mio,
O my victory, O my treasure will-be, O beloved my,
(O my victory, O you will be my treasure, O my beloved,)

O mio sol pensiero, E dammi un bacio e il mondo intiero,
O my only thought, And give-me a kiss and the world entire,
(O my only thought, And give me a kiss and the entire world,)

E mi farai tosto obbliar!
And me will-make quickly to-forget!
(And it will make me forget everything!)

Puccini
Avanti Urania!
Forward Urania!

Io non ho l'ali, eppur quando dal molo
I not have the-wings, yet when from-the pier
(I don't have wings, yet when from the pier)

Lancio la prora al mar,
I-lance the bow to-the sea,
(I throw my bow to the sea,)

Fermi gli alcioni sul potente volo
Stop the kingfishers on-the potent flight
(The kingfishers stop in their mighty flight)

Si librano a guardar. Io non ho pinne,
Them they-hover to watch. I not have fins,
(as they hover to watch. I don't have fins,)

eppur quando i marosi Niun legno osa affrontar,
yet when the billows No-one ship dares to-affront,
(yet no other boat dares to face the billows,)

Trepidando, gli sguali ardimentosi Mi guardano passar!
Anxiously, the sharks bold Me they-watch passing!
(Anxiously, the bold sharks watch me passing.)

Simile al mio signor,
Like to-the my master,
(Like to my master,)

Mite d'aspetto quanto è forte in cuor,
Mild of-appearance as is strong in heart,
(as mild of appearance as is strong in heart,)

Le fiamme ho anch'io nel petto, Anch'io di spazio,
The flames have also-I in-the breast, Also-I of space,
(I also have flames in my breast, also of space,)

Anch'io di gloria ho smania, Avanti Urania!!
Also-I of glory have desire, Forward Urania!!
(Also I desire glory, Forward Urania!!)

Canto d'anime, Pagina d'Album
Song of-souls, Page of-Album

Fuggon gli anni gli inganni e le chimere
Flee the years the deceits and the illusions
(The years, the deceits and the illusions flee)

Cadon recisi i fiori e le speranze
They-fall short the flowers and the hopes
(Flowers and hopes are cut short)

In vane e tormentose disianze
In vain and tormented desires
(In vain and tormented desires)

Svaniscon le mie brevi primavere.
They-vanish the my brief springs.
(My brief springs vanish.)

Ma vive e canta ancora forte e solo
But lives and sings still strong and alone
(But an ideal lives and sings still strong and alone)

Nelle notti del cuore un ideale
In-the nights of-the heart an ideal
(In the nights an ideal of the heart)

Siccome in alta notte siderale
As in deep night starry
(As the solitary nightingale sings)

Inneggia solitario l'usignolo.
Sings solitary the-nightingale.
(in the deep starry night.)

Canta, canta ideal tu solo forte
Sing, sing ideal you alone strong
(Sing, sing, you one strong ideal)

E dalle brume audace eleva il vol lassù,
And from-the mist boldly flies the flight up-there,
(And from the mist boldly flies the flight up there,)

A sfidar l'oblio l'odio la morte
To defy the-oblivion the-hate the death
(To defy oblivion, hate, death)

Dove non son tenèbre e tutto è sol!
Where not are shadows and all is sun!
(Where there are no shadows and all is sunshine!)

Tutto è sol! Tutto è sol!
All is sun! All is sun!
(All is sunshine! All is sunshine!)

(Casa Mia, Casa Mia)
(Home My, Home My)

Casa mia, casa mia Per piccina che tu sia,
Home my, home my For small that you may-be,
(My home, my home, though you may be small,)

Tu mi sembri una Badia, Casa mia,
You me seem an Abbey, Home my,
(To me you seem like an Abbey, my home,)

Per piccina che tu sia Tu mi sembri una Badia,
For small that you may-be You me seem an Abbey,
(For, small that you may be, To me you seem like an Abbey,)

Casa mia, casa mia, casa mia.
Home my, home my, home my.
(My home, my home, my home.)

Puccini
E l'uccellino
And the-little-bird

E l'uccellino canta sulla fronda:
And the-little-bird sings on-the branch:
(And the little bird sings on the branch:)

Dormi tranquillo, boccuccia d'amore;
You-sleep peacefully, dainty of-love;
(Sleep peacefully, dainty love;)

Piegala giù quella testina bionda,
Bend-it down that little-head blond,
(Bend down that little blond head,)

Della tua mamma posala sul cuore.
Of-the your mamma place-it on-the heart.
(Place it on your mother's heart.)

E l'uccellino canta su quel ramo,
And the-little-bird sings on that branch,
(And the little bird sings on that branch,)

Tante cosine belle imparerai,
So-many things beautiful you-will-learn,
(You will learn so many beautiful things,)

Ma se vorrai conoscer quanto'io t'amo,
But if you-want to-know how-I you-love,
(But if you want to know how much I love you,)

Nessuno al mondo potrà dirlo mai!
No-one to-the world will-be-able to-tell-it ever!
(No one in the world will ever be able to tell you!)

E l'uccellino canta al ciel sereno:
And the-little-bird sings to-the heaven serene:
(And the little bird sings to the serene heaven:)

Dormi tesoro mio qui sul mio seno.
You-sleep treasure my here on-the my breast.
(You sleep here on my breast, my treasure.)

Inno a Diana (Ai Cacciatori Italiani)
Hymn to Diana (To-the Hunters Italian)

Gloria a te, se alle notti silenti
Glory to you, if to-the nights silent
(Glory to you, if to the silent nights)

Offri, O Cinzia, i bei raggi all'amor;
You-offer, O Cynthia, the beautiful rays to-the-love;
(You offer, O Cynthia, the beautiful rays of love;)

Gloria a te, se ai meriggi cocenti
Glory to you, if to-the mid-days burning
(Glory to you, if in the hot afternoons)

Tempri, o Diana, dei forti il valor.
You-temper, o Diana, of-the strong-ones the valor.
(You temper, o Diana, the valor of the strong ones.)

Sui tuoi baldi e fedeli seguaci
From-the your bold and faithful followers
(From your bold and faithful followers)

Veglia sempre con l'occhio divin;
Watch always with the-eye divine;
(Always watch with your divine eye;)

Tu li guida alle imprese più audaci,
You them guide to-the deeds most audacious,
(You guide them on the most audacious deeds,)

Li sorreggi nell'aspro cammin.
Them you-sustain in-the-rough path.
(you sustain them on the rough path.)

Dalle vette dell'Alpi nevose
From-the peaks of-the-Alps snowy
(From the peaks of the snowy Alps)

Fino ai lidi del siculo mar;
Until to-the shores of-the Sicilian sea;
(To the shores of the Sicilian sea;)

Per i campi el le selve più ombrose,
Through the fields of the woods most shady,
(Through the fields of the shadiest woods,)

Dove amavi le fiere incontrar;
Where you-loved the fierce-animals to-meet;
(Where you loved to meet the fierce animals;)

Sovra i laghi, ove baciano l'onda
Over the lakes, where kiss the-wave
(Over the lakes, where the wave)

Le corolle di candidi fior,
The petals of white flowers,
(kisses the white flowers' petals,)

Giunga a te, come un'eco profonda,
Come to you, like an-echo profound,
(Come to you, like a profound echo,)

Questo fervido canto d'amor!
This fervid song of-love!
(This fervid song of love!)

Gloria a te, Gloria, Gloria!
Glory to you, Glory, Glory!
(Glory to you, Glory, Glory!)

Inno a Roma
Hymn to Rome

I

Roma divina, a te sul Campidoglio
Rome divine, to you on-the Capital
(Divine Rome, to you from the Capital)

Dove eterno verdeggia il sacro alloro,
Where eternally green the sacred laurel,
(Where the sacred laurel is eternally green,)

A te, nostra fortezza e nostro orgoglio,
To you, our force and our pride,
(To you, our force and our pride,)

    Ascende il coro.
    Ascends the chorus.
    (The chorus ascends.)

Salve, Dea Roma! Ti sfavilla in fronte
Hail, Goddess Rome! You sparkle in brow
(Hail, Goddess Rome! On your brow sparkles)

Il sol che nasce sulla nuova storia.
The sun that born on-the new age.
(The sun that is born on the new age.)

Fulgida in arme all'ultimo orizzonte,
Shining in arms to-the-last horizon,
(Shining in arms to the last horizon,)

    Sta la Vittoria.
    Stays the Victory.
    (The Victory is held.)

Sole che sorgi libero e giocondo,
Sun that rises free and happy,
(Sun that rises free and happy,)

Sul Colle nostro i tuoi cavalli doma:
On-the Hills our the your horses tame:
(On our hills, stop your horses:)

Tu non vedrai nessuna cosa al mondo
You not will-see no thing to-the world
(You will not see anything in the world)

> Maggior di Roma.
> Greather than Rome.
> (Greater that Rome.)

II

Per tutto il cielo è un volo di bandiere
In all in heaven is a flight of banner
(In all the heavens banners are flying)

E la pace del mondo oggi è latina.
And the peace of-the world today is Latin.
(And today the peace of the world is Latin.)

I tricolore canta sul cantiere,
The tri-colors sing on-the shipyard,
(The Italian flag sings in the shipyard,)

> Su l'officina.
> On the-workshop.
> (Above the workshop.)

Madre di messi e di lanosi armenti;
Mother of harvests and of woolly flocks;
(Mother of harvest and of woolly flocks;)

D'opere schiette e di pensose scuole,
Of-works frank and of thoughtful schools,
(Of genuine works and of thoughtful schools,)

Tornano alle tue case i Reggimenti
Return to-the your houses the Regiments
(Return the regiment to your houses)

E sorge il sole.
And rise the sun.
(And the sun rises.)

Sole che sorgi libero e giocondo,
Sun that rises free and happy,
(Sun that rises free and happy,)

Sul Colle nostro i tuoi cavalli doma:
On-the Hills our the your horses tame:
(On our hills, stop your horses:)

Tu non vedrai nessuna cosa al mondo
You not will-see no thing to-the world
(You will not see anything in the world)

Maggior di Roma.
Greater than Rome.
(Greater than Rome.)

Puccini
Mantìa l'avviso
False the-warning

Mentìa l'avviso...Eppur d'Ausena è questa
False the-warning...Yet of-Ausena is this
(The warning was false...Yet this is the august valley)

L'angusta valle...e qui fatal dimora
The-august valley...and here fatal abode
(of Ausena...and here the fatal abode)

Mi presagiva la segreta voce
To-me predicted the secret voice
(To me predicted the secret voice)

Che turba da più notti il mio riposo, il mio riposo.
That disturbed of more nights the my repose, the my repose,
(That disturbed my repose for many nights, my repose,)

Tu cui nomar non oso,
You whom to-name not I-dare,
(You whom I dare not name,)

Tu! funesta donna, dall'avel risorta
You! sorrowful woman, from-the-tomb risen
(You! sorrowful woman, risen from the tomb)

Per mio supplizio, un'altra volta ancora
For me supplication, another time again
(At my supplication, once again)

Promettesti vedermi...e in rio momento.
Promised-you to-see-me...and in wicked moment.
(You promised to see me...and in a wicked moment.)

Ah! chi geme?...M'inganno...
Ah! who moans?...Me-I-deceive...
(Ah! who moans?...I'm mistaken...)

è l'onda, è il vento.
is the-wave, is the wind.
it is the wave, it is the wind.

E la notte che mi reca Le sue larve, i suoi timori,
Is the night that me brings The its ghosts, the its fears,
(It is the night which brings me its ghosts and its fears,)

Che gli accenti punitori Del rimorso udir mi fa.
That the words punishing Of-the remorse to-hear me makes.
(That makes me hear the punishing words of remorse.)

Puccini
Morire?
To-Die?

Morire?...e chi lo sa qual'è la vita!
To-Die?...and who it knows what-is the life!
(To die?...and who knows what life is!)

Questa che s'apre luminosa e schietta
This that itself-opens bright and sincere
(This that opens itself bright and sincere)

Ai fascini, agli amore, alle speranze,
To-the charms, to-the love, to-the hopes,
(To charms, to love, to hopes,)

O quella che in rinuncie s'è assopita?
O that which in renunciations it-is drowsing?
(Or that one which in renunciations is drowsing?)

E la semplicità timida e queta
Is the simplicity timid and quiet
(It is the timid and quiet simplicity)

Che si tramanda come ammonimento
That so given like a-warning
(That so given like a warning)

Come un segreto di virtú segreta
Like a secret of virtue hidden
(Like a secret of hidden virtue)

Perchè ognuno raggiunga la sua mèta,
Why each reaches the its goal,
(So that each reaches his goal,)

O non piuttosto il vivo balenare
Or not rather the lively to-flash
(Or not rather the lively to flash)

Di sogni nuovi sovra sogni stanchi,
Of dreams new on dreams tired,
(Of new dreams on tired dreams,)

E la pace travolta e l'inesausta fede
And the peace upset and the-inexhaustable faith
(And upset peace and the inexhaustable faith)

d'avere per desiderare?
of-having to desire?
(of having desire?)

Ecco io non lo so, ma voi che siete all'altra sponda
Here-is I not it know, but you who are at-the-other bank
(Here I do not know, but you who are on the other bank)

Sulla riva immensa ove fiorisce il fiore della vita
On-the shore immense where flowers the flower of-the life
(On the immense shore where the flower of life blooms)

Son certo lo saprete.
I-am certain it you-will-know.
(I am certain you will know it.)

Puccini
Salve Regina
Hail Queen

Salve, salve del ciel regina, Madre degli infelici,
Hail, hail of-the heaven queen, Mother of-the unfortunates,
(Hail, hail queen of heaven, Mother of the unfortunate ones,)

Stella del mar divin,
Star of-the sea divine,
(Divine star of the sea,)

Stella del mar dall'immortal fulgor, salve.
Star of-the sea of-the-immortal brightness, hail.
(Immortally bright star of the sea, hail.)

Tu accogli e benedici D'ogni sventura il pianto
You accept and bless Of-every unfortunate-one the cry
(You accept and bless the cry of every unfortunate one)

D'un' sguardo Tuo fai santo Ogni terreno amor,
With-a glance You make holy Every earthly love,
(With a glance you make every earthly love holy,)

D'uno sguardo Tuo fai santo Ogni terreno amor.
With-a glance You make holy Every earthly love.
(With a glance you make every earthly love holy.)

Sole e Amore
Sun and Love

Il sole allegramente batte ai tuoi vetri;
The sun joyfully taps at-the your windows;
(The sun joyfully taps at your windows;)

Amor pian pian batte al tuo cuore
Love soft soft taps at-the your heart
(Love softly softly taps at your heart)

E l'uno e l'altro chiama.
And the-one and the-other it-calls.
(And calls one and the other.)

Il sole dice: "O dormente mostrati che sei bella!"
The sun says: "O sleeper show-you that you-are beautiful!"
(The sun says: "O sleeper show how beautiful you are!")

Dice l'amor: "Sorella, col tuo primo pensier
Says the-love: "Sister, with-the your first thought
(Says love: "Sister, with your first thought)

Pensa a chi t'ama!
Think to who you-loves!
(Think of the one who loves you!)

Pensa a chi t'ama! Pensa!"
Think to who you-loves! Think!"
(Think of the one who loves you! Think!")

Al Paganini, G. Puccini.
To Paganini, G. Puccini.
(To Paganini, G. Puccini.)

Puccini
Storiella d'amore (Melodia)
Little-story of-love (Melody)

Noi leggevamo insieme un giorno per diletto
We were-reading together one day for delight
(We were reading together one day for pleasure)

Una gentile istoria piena di mesti amor;
A gentle story full of sad love;
(A pleasant story full of sad love;)

E senz'alcun sospetto ella sedeami a lato,
And without-any doubt she sat-down-me by side,
(And without-any doubt she sat down beside me,)

Sul libro avventurato intenta il guardo e il cor.
On-the book fortunate intent the glance and the heart.
(Her glance and her heart intent on the fortunate book.)

Noi leggevamo insieme, Ah! Ah!
We were-reading together, Ah! Ah!
(We were reading together, Ah! Ah!)

L'onda de' suoi capelli il volto a me lambia,
The-wave of-the her hair the face to me brushed,
(The wave of her hair brushed my face,)

Eco alla voce mia, Eco faceano i suoi sospir.
Echoing to-the voice my, Echoing made-them the her sighs.
(Echoing to my voice, Echoing her sighs.)

Gli occhi dal libro alzando Nel suo celeste viso,
The eyes from-the book I-rose In-the her heavenly face,
(Raising my eyes from the book, In her heavenly face,)

Io vidi in un sorriso Riflesso il mio desir.
I saw in a smile Reflected the my desire.
(I saw my desire reflected in a smile.)

La bella mano al core strinsi di gioia ansante...
The beautiful hand to-the heart pressed of joy panting...
(With panting joy her beautiful hand I pressed to my heart...)

Nè più leggemmo avante...E cadde il libro al suol.
Nor more we-read after...And fell the book to-the soil.
(We read no more...And the book fell to the ground.)

Noi leggevamo insieme, Ah! Ah!
We were-reading together, Ah! Ah!
(We were reading together, Ah! Ah!)

Un lungo, ardente bacio congiunse i labbri aneli,
A long, ardent kiss united the lips yearning,
(A long, ardent kiss united our yearning lips,)

E ad ignorati cieli L'alme spiegaro il vol.
And to-the ignored heavens The-souls unfolded the flight.
(And to the ignored heavens our souls unfolded in flight.)

Puccini
Terra e Mare
Earth and Sea

I pioppi, curvati dal vento,
The poplars, bent by-the wind,
(The poplars, bent by the wind,)

Rimugghiano in lungo filare.
Roar in long rows.
(Roar in long rows.)

Dal buio, tra il sonno, li sento
Of-the darkness, among the sleep, them I-feel
(In the darkness, in my sleep, I hear them)

E sogno la voce del mar.
And I-dream the voice of-the sea.
(And I dream of the voice of the sea.)

E sogno la voce profonda
And I-dream the voice profound
(And I dream of the profound voice)

Dai placidi ritmi possenti;
Of-the placid rhythms powerful;
(Of the placid powerful rhythms;)

Mi guardan, specchiate dall'onda,
Me they-watch, mirrored of-the-wave,
(Mirrored on the wave, the stars)

Le stelle nel cielo fulgenti.
The stars in-the heaven bright.
(in the bright heaven watch me.)

Ma il vento più forte tempesta,
But the wind more strong rages,
(But the wind more strongly rages,)

De' pioppi nel lungo filare,
Of-the poplars in-the long rows,
(In the long rows of the poplars,)

Dal sonno giocondo mi desta...
Of-the sleep happy me awakes...
(It awakes me from my happy sleep...)

Lontana è la voce del mar!
Far-away is the voice of-the sea!
(Far away is the voice of the sea!)

Rossini
Aragonese
Aragonese

Mi lagnerò tacendo della mia sorte amara;
Me I-will-complain silently of-the my fate bitter;
(I will silently complain of my bitter fate;)

ma ch'io non t'ami, o cara, non lo sperar da me.
but that-I not you-love, o dear, not it to-think of me.
(but that I don't love you, o dear, don't think it of me.)

Crudel! In che t'offesi? Farmi penar, perché?
Cruel-one, In that you-propose? Make-me to-suffer, why?
(Cruel one, is that what you propose? why make me suffer?)

Arietta all'antica
Little-Aria in the Old Style

Mi lagnerò tacendo della mia sorte amara;
Me I-will-complain silently of-the my fate bitter;
(I will silently complain of my bitter fate;)

ma ch'io non t'ami, o cara, non lo sperar da me.
but that-I not you-love, o dear, not it to-think of me.
(but that I don't love you, o dear, don't think it of me.)

Crudel! In che t'offesi? Farmi penar, perché?
Cruel-one, In that you-propose? Make-me to-suffer, why?
(Cruel one, is that what you propose? why make me suffer?)

Rossini
Ave Maria
Hail Mary

A te, che benedetta fra tutte sei, Maria,
To you, who blessed among all is, Mary,
(To you, who is blessed among all, Mary,)

voli la prece mia, pura s'innalzia a te.
flies the prayer my, pure itslf-raises to you.
(flies my prayer, pure it raises to you.)

Maria, Maria, la prece mia, s'innalzi a te. Ah!
Mary, Mary, the prayer my, itself-raises to you. Ah!
(Mary, Mary, my prayer raises to you. Ah!)

Si, del mio cammino sii la propizia stella.
Yes, in-the my path be the favorable star.
(Yes, may the favorable star be in my path.)

Per venir teco, bella, sarà la morte a me.
To come you-with, beautiful-one, will-be the death to me.
(To be with you, beautiful one, death will come to me.)

A te...pura Maria.
To you...pure Mary.
(To you...pure Mary.)

Il Rimprovero
The Reproach

Mi lagnerò tacendo della mia sorte amara, ah!
Me I-will-complain silently of-the my fate bitter, ah!
(I will silently complain of my bitter fate, ah!)

ma ch'io non t'ami, o cara, non lo sperar da me.
but that-I not you-love, o dear, not it to-think of me.
(but that I don't love you, o dear, don't think that of me.)

Crudel, perchè fin'ora farmi penar così?
Cruel-one, why till-now make-me suffer thus?
(Cruel one, why make me suffer like this up till now?)

Rossini
L'esule
The-exile

Qui sempre ride il cielo, qui verde ognor la fronda,
Here always laughs the heaven, here green always the branch,
(Here the heavens always laugh, here the branch is always
green,)

qui del ruscello l'onda dolce mi scorre al pie';
here of-the brook the-wave sweet me runs to-the foot;
(here the sweet wave of the brook laps at my feet;)

ma questo suol non è la Patria mia.
but this soil not is the Fatherland my.
(but this soil is not my Fatherland.)

Qui nell'azzurro flutto sempre si specchia il sole:
Here in-the-blue wave always itself mirrors the sun:
(Here the sun is always mirrored in the blue wave:)

i gigli e le viöle crescono intorno a me;
the lilies and the violets grow around to me;
(the lilies and violets grow around me;)

ma questo suol non è la Patria mia.
but this soil not is the Fatherland my.
(but this soil is not my Fatherland.)

Le vergini son vaghe come le fresche rose che
The virgins are pretty like the fresh roses that
(The virgins are pretty like the fresh roses that,)

al loro crin compose amor pegno di fe';
to-the their hair compose love pledged of faith;
(placed in their hair, pledge faithful love;)

ma questo suol non è la Patria mia.
but this soil not is the Fatherland my.
(but this soil is not my Fatherland.)

Nell'Itale contrade è una città Regina;
In-the-Italian districts is a city Queen;
(In the Italian districts is a Queen city;)

la Ligure marina sempre le bagna il pie' La ravvisate,
the Ligurian marina always them wets the foot It recognized,
(the Ligurian marina always wets the recognized foot,)

ell'è la Patria mia.
she-is the Fatherland my.
(that is my Fatherland.)

La Patria mia, la Patria mia ell'è.
The Fatherland my, the Fatherland my she-is.
(My Fatherland, my Fatherland is she.)

Rossini
L'Invito
The-Invitation

Vieni, o Ruggiero, la tua Eloisa da te divinsa no,
Come, o Ruggiero, the your Eloisa of you plans no,
(Come, o Ruggiero, your Eloisa plans not to,)

non può restar:
not can stay:
(cannot stay with you:)

alle mie lacrime già rispondevi,
to-the my tears already reply-you,
(you already reply to my tears,)

vieni, ricevi il mio pregar.
come, receive the my prayer.
(come, receive my prayer.)

Vieni, o bell'angelo, vien, mio diletto,
Come, o beautifu¹-angel, come, my delight,
(Come, o beautiful angel, come, my delight,)

sovra il mio petto vieni a posar!
on the my breast come to rest!
(come onto my breast to rest!)

Senti se palpita, se amor t'invita...
Feel if it-palpitates, if love you-it-invites...
(Feel if it palpitates, if it invites you to love...)

vieni, mia vita, vien, vieni, fammi spirar.
come, my life, come, come, make-me expire.
(come, my life, come, come, make me die.)

L'Orgia
The-Debauch

Amiamo, cantiamo le donne e i liquor,
Let-us-love, let-us-sing the women and the liquor,
(Let's love, let's sing to women and liquor,)

gradita è la vita fra Bacco ed Amor!
welcome is the life among Bacchus and Eros!
(life among Bacchus and Eros is welcome!)

Se Amore ho nel core,
If Love I-have in-the heart,
(If I have love in my heart,)

ho il vin nella testa, che gioia, che festa,
I-have the wine in-the head, what joy, what festival,
(I have wine in my head, what fun, what a party,)

che amabile ardor! Amando, scherzando, trincando liquor,
such amiable ardor! Loving, joking, drinking liquor,
(such amiable ardor! Loving, joking, drinking liquor,)

m'avvampo, mi scampo da noie e dolor.
me-excited, me saves from weariness and sorrow.
(excited me, saves me from weariness and sorrow.)

Cantiam...
Let-us-sing...
(Let's sing...)

gradita è la vita fra Bacco ed Amor.
welcome is the life among Bacchus and Eros.
(life among Bacchus and Eros is welcome.)

Danziamo, cantiamo, alziamo il bicchier,
Let-us-dance, let-us-sing, let-us-raise the glass,
(Let's dance, let's sing, let's raise our glasses,)

ridiam, sfidiam i tristi pensier, amando, scherzando,
let-us-laugh, let-us-defy the sad thoughts, loving, joking,
(let's laugh, let's defy sad thoughts, loving, joking,)

trincando liquor, m'avvampo,
drinking liquor, me-excites,
(drinking liquor, excites me,)

mi scampo da noie e dolor....
me saves from weariness and sorrow....
(saves me from weariness and sorrow....)

Regina divina la madre d'Amor giuliva
Queen divine the mother of-Eros joyful
(The divine queen mother of Eros joyfully)

rinnova ogni cor...balzante,
you-renew every heart...leaping,
(renews every heart...leaping,)

spumante con vivo bollor
foaming with living excitement
(foaming with living excitement)

è il vino divino del mondo signor...
is the wine divine of-the world sir...
(wine is divine in the world, sir...)

Già ballo, traballo, che odor, che vapor!
Already I-dance, I-stagger, what scent, what aroma!
(Already I dance, I stagger, what a smell, what an aroma!)

si beva, ribeva con sacro furor.
one drinks, re-drinks with holy fury.
(one drinks, drinks again with holy fury.)

Cantiam...la vita è compita fra Bacco ed Amor.
Let-us-sing...the life is fulfilled among Bacchus and Eros.
(Let's sing...life if fulfilled among Bacchus and Eros.)

Evviva le donne e il liquor!
Long-live the women and the liquor!
(Long live women and liquor!)

Già ballo, traballo, che odor, che vapor!
Already I-dance, I-stagger. what scent, what odor!
(Already I dance, I stagger, what a smell, what an aroma!)

Rossini
L'ultima ricordo
The-last remembrance

Odi un uom che muore, odi l'estremo suon
Hear a man who is-dying, hear the last sound
(Hear a man who is dying, hear his last sound)

quest'appassito fiore ti lascio Olimpia in don.
this-faded flower to-you I-leave Olimpia as gift.
(I leave this faded flower to you Elvira as a gift.)

Quanto prezioso ei sia.
How precious he is.
(How precious he is.)

Tu lo conosci appien dal dì che fosti mia
You it know fully from-the day which you-were mine
(From the day which you were mine, you know it fully,)

te l'involai dal sen.
you it-I-stole from-the breast.
(From your breast I stole it.)

Premio fu allor d'affetto, or pegno di dolore
Symbol was then of-affection, now pledge of sorrow
(That faded flower, once a symbol of affection,)

torni ad ornarti il petto questo appassito fior.
returns to place-you the breast that faded flower.
(returns to your breast, now as a pledge of sorrow.)

La Danza
The Dance

Già la luna è in mezzo al mare, mamma mia, si salterà;
Already the moon is in half on-the sea, dear me, itself skips;
(Already the moon is half set on the sea, oh my, skipping
itself;)

l'ora è bella per danzare,
the-hour is beautiful for dancing,
(the hour is beautiful for dancing,)

chi è in amor non mancherà.
who is in love not will-it-miss.
(anyone in love will not miss it.)

Già la luna è in mezzo al mare, mamma mia, si salterà.
Already the moon is in half on-the sea, dear me, itself skips;
(Already the moon is half set on the sea, oh my, skipping
itself;)

Presto in danza a tondo, donne mie, venite qua,
Quick in dance to turn, ladies my, come here,
(Quickly spin in a dance, my ladies, come here,)

un garzon bello e gioconco a ciascuna toccherà.
a boy beautiful and playful to everyone will-have-a-turn.
(a beautiful and playful boy will have a spin with everyone.)

Finchè in ciel brilla una stella, e la luna splenderà,
Until in heaven sparkles a star, and the moon will-shine,
(Until a star sparkles in heaven, and the moon will shine,)

il più bel con la più bella
the most beautiful-boy with the most beautiful-girl
(the most beautiful boy and girl)

tutta notte danzerà.
all night will-dance.
(will dance all night.)

Mamma mia, già la luna...frinche...la ra, la ra....
Dear me, already the moon...already...la ra, la ra....
(Oh my, already the moon...already...la ra, la ra....)

Salta, gira, ogni coppia a cerchio va, già s'avanza,
Leap, turn, every couple to circle go, already it-advances,
(Leap, turn, every couple have a turn, already it advances,)

si ritira, e all'assalto tornerà.
it withdraws, and to-the-excitement will-return.
(it withdraws, and returns to the excitement.)

Serra colla bionda, colla bruna va qua e là,
Press with-the blonde, with-the brunette go here and there,
(Dance with the blond, with the brunette of here and there,)

colla rossa va a seconda,
with-the redhead go to second,
(go second with the redhead,)

colla smorta fermo sta.
with-the pale-one still she-remains.
(with the pale one, she still remains.)

Viva il ballo a tondo, sono un re, sono un bascià,
Hail the dance to turn, I-am a king, I-am a lord,
(Hail the turning dance, I am a king, I am a lord,)

è il piu bel piacer del mondo,
is the most beautiful pleasure of-the world,
(it is the most beautiful pleasure of the world,)

la più cara volutta.
the most dear voluptousness.
(the dearest desire.)

La fioraia fiorentina
The flowergirl florentine

I più bei fior comprate, fanciulle amanti e spose:
The most beautiful flowers buy, maidens loving and spouses:
(Buy my most beautiful flowers, loving maidens and spouses:)

son fresche le mie rose, non spiran che l'amor,
they-are fresh the my roses, not they-die like the-love,
(my roses are fresh, they don't die like love,)

no, no, non spiran che l'amor. Ahimè!
no, no, not they-die like the-love. Alas!
(no, no, they don't die like love. Alas!)

Soccorso implora mia madre, poveretta,
Help implores my mother, poor-thing,
(My mother implores help, poor thing,)

e da me sola aspetta del pan
and from me alone she-awaits of-the bread
(and on me alone she depends for bread)

e non dell'or. Ahimè! Ah!
and not of-the-gold. Alas! Ah!
(and not for gold. Alas! Ah!)

Rossini
La gita in gondola
The trip in gondola

Voli l'agile barchetta, voga, o marinar, or ch'Elvira
Flies the-agile little-boat, row, oh sailor, now that-Elvira
(The little agile boat flies, row, oh sailor, now that my)

mia diletta a me in braccio sfida il mar.
my delight to me in arms challenges the sea.
(delight, Elvira, in my arms, challenges the sea.)

Brilla in calma la laguna, una vela non appar,
Sparkles in calm the lagoon, a sail not appear,
(The calm lagoon sparkes, a sail doesn't appear,)

pallidetta è in ciel la luna,
somewhat-pale is in sky the moon,
(the sky is somewhat pale,)

tutto invita a sospirar.
everything it-invites to sigh.
(inviting everything to sigh.)

Voga, voga, marinar. Se ad un bacio amor t'invita, non temer,
Row, row, sailor. If to a kiss love you-invites, not be-afraid,
(Row, row, sailor. If love invites you to a kiss, don't be
afraid,)

mio bel tesor, tu saprai che sia la vita
my beautiful treasure, you will-know that is the life
(my beautiful treasure, only in the kiss of love)

sol nel bacio dell'amor.
only in-the kiss of-the-love.
(will you know life.)

Ma già un zeffiro sereno dolce ondeggia il mar...
But already a breeze serene sweet undulates the sea...
(But already a sweet serene breeze undulates the sea...)

vieni, Elvira, a questo seno, vieni, e apprendi a palpitar...
come, Elvira, to this breast, come, and learn to palpitate...
(come, Elvira, to this breast, come, and learn to palpitate...)

voga, voga, marinar.
row, row, sailor.
(row, row, sailor.)

Rossini
La lontananza
The distance

Quando dal tuo verone,
When from-the your balcony,
(When from you balcony,)

fra l'ombre della sera,
among the-shadows of-the evening,
(among the evening shadows,)

la fìebile canzone sciorrà la capinera
the mournful songs will-pour-out the blackcap
(from the blackcap mournful songs will pour out)

ed una pura stella
and a clear star
(and a clear star)

nel suo gentil passaggio la fronte tua
in-the your gentle passage the face your
(will brighten your gentle path and a ray of light)

sì bella rischiarerà d'un raggio,
so beautiful will-brighten by-a ray,
(will brighten your beautiful face)

quando il ruscel d'argento gemere udrai vicino
when the brook of-silver laments you-will-hear near
(when the silver brook laments, you will hear nearby)

e sospirar il vento e susurrare il pino, deh!
and sighing the wind and murmurring the pine, ah!
(the sighing wind and the murmurring pine, ah!)

ti rammenta, o sposa, che quello è il mio saluto.
you it-remembers, o spouse, that that is the my greeting.
(it remembers you, o wife, that is my greeting.)

Donami allor pietosa di lacrime un tributo e pensa,
Give-me then pitiful of tears a tribute and it-thinks,
(Then sad, give me a piteous, tearful tribute and it thinks,)

o Elvira mia, che il povero cantor per mezzo lor t'invia
o Elvira my, that the poor singer by means them you-it-sends
(o my Elvira, that the poor singer, by singing, sends you)

sempre più fido il cor.
always more faithful the heart.
(always the heart more faithful.)

Rossini
La Partenza
The Parting

Ecco quel fiero istante, Nice, mia Nice, addio;
Here-is that severe moment, Nice, my Nice, goodbye;
(Here is that harsh moment, Nice, my Nice, goodbye;)

come vivrò, ben mio, così lontan da te?
how I-will-live, beloved my, this far from you?
(how will I live, my beloved, so far from you?)

Io vivrò sempre in pene, io non avrò più bene,
I will-live always in pain, I not will-have more good,
(I will always live in pain, no more good will come to me,)

e tu chi sa se mai ti sovverrai di me!
and you who knows if ever you will-remember of me!
(and you who knows if ever you will remember me!)

Sempre nel tuo cammino, sempre m'avrai vicino
Always in-the your path, always me-you-will-have near
(Always in your path, you will always have me near you)

e tu chi sa se mai ti sovverrai di me!
and you who knows if ever you will-remember of me!
(and you who knows if ever you will remember me!)

La Pastorella delle Alpi
The Shepherdess of-the Alps

Son bella pastorella, che scende ogni mattino,
I-am beautiful shepherdess, who descends every morning,
(I am the beautiful shepherdess, who descends every
morning,)

ed offre un cestellino di fresche frutta e fior.
and offers a small-basket of fresh fruit and flowers.
(and offers a small basket of fresh fruit and flowers.)

Chi viene al primo albore avrà vezzose rose
Who comes at-the first dawn will-have pretty roses
(He who comes at dawn will have pretty roses)

e poma rugiadose, venite al mio giardin.
and apple dewy, come to-the my garden.
(and dewy apples, come into my garden.)

Ahu...Ahu...a...a....
Ahu...Ahu...ah...ah....
(Ahu...Ahu...ah...ah....)

Chi nel notturno orrore smarrì la buona via,
Who in-the nightly horror loses the right way,
(He who in the horrible night loses his way,)

alla capanna mia ritroverà il cammin.
in-the hut my will-find-again the way.
(in my hut will refind his way.)

Venite, o passaggiero, la pastorella è qua,
Come, o passerby, the shephardess is here,
(Come, o passerby, the shephardess is here,)

ma il fior del suo pensiero ad uno sol darà!
but the flower of-the her thought to one only she-will-give!
(But to only one will she give the flower of her thought!)

Rossini
La Promessa
The Promise

Ch'io mai vi possa lasciar d'amare,
That-I never you be-able to-stop from-loving,
(That I will never be able to stop loving you,)

no, nol credete, pupille care;
no, not-it you-believe, eyes dear;
(no, don't you believe it, dear eyes;)

nemmen per gioco v'ingannerò.
not-even to joke you-I-would-deceive.
(not even as a joke would I deceive you.)

Voi sole siete le mie faville,
You only are the my sparks,
(You alone are my sparks,)

e voi sarete, care pupille,
and you will-be, dear eyes,
(and you will be, dear eyes,)

il mio bel foco sin ch'io vivrò, Ah!
the my beautiful fire until that-I will-live, Ah!
(my beautiful fire as long as I live, Ah!)

Musique Anodine
Soothing Music

Mi lagnerò tacendo della mia sorte amara;
Me I-will-complain silently of-the my fate bitter;
(I will silently complain of my bitter fate;)

ma ch'io non t'ami, o cara, non lo sperar da me.
but that-I not you-love, o dear, not it to-think of me.
(but that I don't love you, o dear, don't think it of me.)

Crudel! In che t'offesi? Farmi penar, perché?
Cruel-one, In that you-propose? Make-me to-suffer, why?
(Cruel one, is that what you propose? why make me suffer?)

Rossini
La Regata Veneziana
The Venetian Regatta

1. **Anzoleta avanti la regata**
1. Little-Angel before the regatta

(Venetian Dialect:)

Là su la machina xe la bandiera, varda, la vedistu,
There on the boat is the flag, look, it do-you-see,
(There is the flag on the boat, look, do you see it,)

vala a ciapar. Co quela tornime in qua sta sera,
go-there to get. With that return-to-me in here this evening,
(go there to get it. Come back to me here with it,)

o pur a sconderte ti pol andar.
or now to hide yourself then to-go.
(or now go to hide yourself.)

In pope, Momolo, no te incantar.
In stern, Momolo, not you be-enchanted.
(Get in the stern, Momolo, don't be distracted.)

Va, voga d'anema la gondoleta,
Go, row with-soul the little-gondola,
(Go, row with vigor the little gondola,)

nè el primo premio te pol mancar,
nor the first prize to-you can miss,
(or the first prize can pass you by,)

va là, recordite la to Anzoleta
go there, remember the your little-Angel
(go there, remember your little Angel)

che da sto pergolo te sta a vardar.
who from this pergola you stay to watch.
(who is watching you from this pergola.)

In pope, Momolo, no te incantar, cori a svolar.
In stern, Momolo, not you be-enchanted, run to fly.
(Get in the stern, Momolo, don't you be distracted, run as if
flying.)

1. Little-Angel before of the regatta

(Italian:)

Sul palco sventola gran la bandiera, guarda, sì guardala,
On-the platform waved-it big the flag, look, if you-see-it,
(On the platform waves the big flag, look, if you see it,)

valla a pigliar.
go-there to take.
(go there and take it.)

Hai a recarmela prima di sera,
You-have to take-me-it before of evening,
(You must bring it to me before evening,)

o più tra gli uomini non ti mostrar.
or more among the men not you to-show.
(or no longer show yourself among men.)

In poppa, Momolo, non indugiar. Va, voga,
In stern, Momolo, not you-be-enchanted. Go, row,
(Get in the stern, Momolo, don't be distracted. Go, row,)

spingila la gondoletta, nè il primo premio ti può mancar,
push-it the little-gondola, nor the first prize to-you can miss,
(push the little gondola, or the first prize can pass you by,)

va là, ricordati la tua diletta
go there, remember the your beloved
(go there, remember your beloved)

che in ansia trepida ti sta a guardar.
who in anxiety trembling you stay to watch.
(who is watching you in trembling anxiety.)

In poppa, Momolo, non indugiar, corri a volar.
In stern, Momolo, don't you-be-enchanted, run as flying
(Get into the stern, Momolo, don't be distracted, run as if flying.)

Rossini
La Regata Veneziana
The Venetian Regatta

2. **Anzoleta co passa la regata**
2. Little-Angel with it-passes the regatta

(Venetian Dialect:)

I xe qua, vardeli, povereti i ghe da drento,
I stay here, look-at-them, poor-ones I who from thirty,
(I remain here, looking at them, poor fellows who are thirsty,)

ah contrario tira el vento, i gha l'acqua in so favor.
ah contrary blows the wind, I that the-water in their favor.
(ah the wind blows contrary, the water is in their favor.)

El mio Momolo dov'elo? ah lo vedo, el xe secondo.
The my Momolo where-is-he? ah him I-see, he is second.
(Where is my Momolo? ah I see him, he is second.)

Ah! che smania! mi confondo,
Ah! what craving! I-am confused,
(Ah! what desire! I'm confused,)

a tremar me sento el cuor.
to tremble me I-feel the heart.
(I feel my heart trembling.)

Su coragio, voga, prima d'esser al paleto se ti voghi,
Go-ahead courage, row, before being at-the pole it you row,
(Go with courage, row, row it to the pole,)

ghe scometo, tutti indrio ti lassarà.
that I-bet, everybody behind to will-leave.
(that I'll bet, leaving everyone behind.)

Caro, par che ei svola, el li magna tuti quanti,
Dear, it-seems that he flies, he them eats all everyone,
(Dear, it seems that he flies, he passes them all,)

meza barca l'è andà avanti, ah capisso, el m'a vardà.
half boat of-him goes in-front, ah I-understand, he me-is watching.
(he's a half boat ahead, ah I understand, he's watching me.)

2. Anzoleta co passa la regata
2. Little-Angel with it-passes the regatta

(Italian:)

Sono qua, non vedi? curvi stanno in sovra al remo,
I-am here, not you-see? curved they-are in upon the oar,
(I'm here, don't you see? they're bent over the oars,)

ahi la meta è ancor lontana, gira il vento a tramontana,
ah the goal is still far, turns the wind of North,
(ah the goal is still far, the wind turns to the North,)

poveretti, io tutta tremo, la corrente è in lor favor.
poor-them, I all-over tremble, the current is in their favor,
(poor fellows, I tremble all over, the current is in their favor,)

Il mio Momolo l'hai visto? or lo scorgo,
The my Momolo him-you-have seen? now him I-notice,
(Did you see my Momolo? now I notice him,)

egli è secondo. Ah! che smania! mi confondo, ahi!
he is second. Ah! what anxiety! me I-confused, ah!
(he is second. Ah! what anxiety! I'm confused,)

balzar mi sento il cor.
to-jump me I-feel the heart.
(ah! my heart feels like jumping.)

Su coraggio, voga, pria di giunger alla meta
Go-ahead courage, row, before of arriving at-the goal
(Go with courage, row, before arriving at the goal)

spiega tutta la tua foga, e nessun ti vincerà.
unfold all the your ardor, and no-one you will-win.
(employ all your ardor, and no one will beat you.)

Caro, par ch'ei voli, li ha passati tutti quanti,
Dear, it-seems that-he flies, them he-has passed all everyone,
(Dear, it seems as if he flies, he has passed them all,)

mezza barca sta davanti, ah comprendo, ei me guardò.
half boat is in-front, ah I-understand, he me looked.
(a half boat ahead, ah I understand, he looked at me.)

Rossini
La Regata Veneziana
The Venetian Regatta

3. **Anzoleta dopo la regata**
3. Little-Angel after the regatta

(Venetian Dialect:)

Ciapa un baso, un altro ancora, caro Momolo, de cuor;
Catch a kiss, an other more, dear Momolo, from heart;
(Take a kiss, another, dear Momolo, from my heart;)

qua destrachite che xe ora de sugarte sto sudor.
here at-the-right-hand that is time to dry-up this sweat.
(here at your right hand it is time to dry your sweat.)

Ah t'ho visto co passando
Ah you-I-have seen with passing
(Ah I have seen you in passing)

su mi l'ocio ti a butà
by my the-eye to-you in throwing
(by throwing my glance toward you)

e godito respitrando: un bel premio el ciaparà...
and enjoyed breathing: a beautiful prize he will-catch...
(and enjoyed whispering: he will catch a beautiful prize...)

sì un bel premio in sta bandiera, che xe rossa de color;
yes a nice prize in this flag, which is red of color;
(yes this flag is a nice prize, which is red;)

gha parlà Venezia intiera, la t'a dito vincitor.
that will-talk Venice entire, it you-have called winner.
(of which all Venice will-talk, you are called the winner.)

Ciapa un baso, benedeto a vogar nissun te pol,
Catch a kiss, blessed in rowing no-one you can,
(Take a kiss, no rower is more blessed than you,)

de casada de tragheto ti xe el megio barcarol.
of last-name of ferry-boat you are the best boatman.
(yours is the best name among rowers of ferryboats.)

(Italian:)

Prendi un bacio, un altro ancora, caro Momolo, di cor;
Take a kiss, an other more, dear Momolo, from heart;
(Take a kiss, another, dear Momolo, from my heart;)

su riposati che è ora ch'io t'asciughi quel sudor.
go-ahead rest-you that is hour that-I you-dry that sweat.
(go ahead and rest because it is time that I dry that sweat.)

Ah t'ho visto, m'hai guardate
Ah you-I-have seen, me-you-have looked
(Ah I have seen you, you looked at me)

sul poggiolo nel passar
on-the balcony in-the passing
(on the balcony in passing)

e pensai racconsolata: un bel premio ei de' pigliar;
and I-thought consoled: a nice prize he to take;
(and consoled, I thought: he will take a nice prize;)

non un sol, Venezia intera ti proclama vincitor.
not just one, Venice entire you it-proclaims winner.
(not just one, but all Venice proclaims you the winner.)

Prende un bacio, benedetto non hai pari nel vogar,
Take a kiss, blessed not you-have equals in-the rowing,
(Take a kiss, more blessed among rowers you have no equals,)

per famiglia per traghetto niun a petto ti può star.
for-the family for ferry-boat no-one at chest your can stay.
(for no one can keep up with you in the family of ferryboat
rowers.)

Rossini
Tirana alla spagnola
Tirana in the Spanish Style

Mi lagnerò tacendo della mia sorte amara;
Me I-will-complain silently of-the my fate bitter;
(I will silently complain of my bitter fate;)

ma ch'io non t'ami, o cara, non lo sperar da me.
but that-I not you-love, o dear, not it to-think of me.
(but that I don't love you, o dear, don't think it of me.)

Crudel! In che t'offesi? Farmi penar, perché?
Cruel-one, In that you-propose? Make-me to-suffer, why?
(Cruel one, is that what you propose? why make me suffer?)

Addio!
Goodbye!

Cadon stanche le foglie al suol,
They-fall tired the leaves to-the soil,
(The tired leaves fall to the soil,)

Bianche strisce serpon sull'onda,
White streaks it-serpents on-the-wave,
(White streaks twist on the wave,)

Lieve nebbia nell-aria fonda,
Soft fog in-the-air bottom,
(Soft fog settles in the air,)

Sembran freddi i rai del sol.
They-resemble cold the rays of-the sun.
(The rays of the sun resemble the cold.)

Le rondinelle lasciano il nido,
The swallows leave the nest,
(Swallows leave their nests,)

Verso altro lido, le trae desio:
Toward other shore, it makes-me wish:
(Toward another shore, it makes me wish:)

Estate, addio! Una voce lontan,
Summer, goodbye! A voice far-away,
(Summer, goodbye! A voice far-away,)

"Odi e impara" sembra gridare,
"Hear and learn" it-seems to-shout,
("Listen and learn" it seems to cry,)

"Non diverso dall'oggi è il doman.
"Not different from-today is the tomorrow.
("Tomorrow is not different from today.)

Gioia e duolo, polve ed altare."
Joy and sorrow, dust and altar."
(Joy and sorrow, dust and altar.")

Ogni legame mortal si spezza,
Every union mortal so breaks,
(Every mortal union thus breaks,)

Copre l'oblio fiele e dolcezza.
Covers the-oblivion bitterness and sweetness.
(Bitterness and sweetness cover the oblivion.)

O speme, addio! Perche aspettar tutor, oh! dolce amor?
O hope, goodbye! Why to-wait-for guardian, oh! sweet love?
(O hope, goodbye! Why wait for a guardian, oh! sweet love?)

Un sol bacio mi dà, posci ten va. Un altro ancor.
A single kiss me it-gave, after you go. An other still.
(One kiss it gave me, then you go. Yet another.)

Pegno d'eterno fè da te voglio,
Pain of-eternal faith by you I-wish,
(I wish by you the eternal pain of faith,)

Perchè il tuo cor è fatalmente mio:
Because the your heart is fatally mine:
(Because your heart is fatally mine:)

Per sempre addio!
For always goodbye!
(Goodbye forever!)

Ancora!
Again!

Il mio pensier, vagano, ti ritrova in mezzo ai fiori,
The my thought, going, you refinds in among to-the flowers,
(My thought, going, finds you among the flowers,)

in un'ombrosa landa del mite aprile a la carezza nova,
in a-shady moor of-the mild April to the caress new,
(in the shady moor of mild April to the new caress,)

ti fanno i rami una gentil ghirlanda.
you make the branches a gentle garland.
(you make a gentle garland of the branches.)

Ma la tua guancia è mesta e scolorita,
But the your cheek is sad and colorless,
(But your cheek is sad and colorless,)

han le tue labbra un languido sospir.
they-have the your lips a languid sigh.
(your lips have a languid sigh.)

Forse tu pure a la trascorsa vita rivolgi,
Perhaps you still to the past life return,
(Perhaps you still return to the past life,)

stanca, il triste sovvenir!
tired, the sad remembrance!
(tired, the sad remembrance!)

O dolce tempo, o rapida stagione,
O sweet time, o rapid season,
(O sweet time, o rapid season,)

con i tuoi raggi a noi più non ritorni!
with the your rays to us more not return!
(to us your rays will no more return!)

Sì breve tacque l'ideal canzone,
So brief quieted the-ideal song,
(So brief quieted the ideal song,)

fuggir veloci i nostri cari giorni!
to-fly quickly the our dear days!
(our dear days fly quickly!)

Ah! vieni a me! Ti stringi al petto ansante,
Ah! come to me! You press to-the breast longed-for,
(Ah! come to me! You press to the longed for breast,)

Fa ch'io m'inebri al caldo tuo sospir!
Make that-I me-you-elate to-the warm your sigh!
(Make me be elated with your warm sigh!)

Baciar potessi ancora, un solo istante,
To-kiss I-could still, a single instant,
(I could still kiss, a single moment,)

la bocca tua suave, e poi morir!
the mouth your sweet, and then die!
(your sweet mouth, and then die!)

Aprile
April

Non senti tu ne l'aria il profumo che spande Primavera?
Not feel you of-it the-air the perfume that pours-out Spring?
(Don't you feel the perfumed air that spring pours out?)

Non senti tu ne l'anima il suon di nove voce lusinghiera?
Not feel you of-it the-soul the sound of new voice favorable?
(Doesn't your soul hear the sound of the new favorable
voice?)

E l'April! E la stagion d'amore! Deh! vieni, o mia gentil,
Is the-April! Is the season of-love! Oh! come, o my gentle,
(It's April! It's the season of love! Oh! come, my gentle one,)

su' prati'n fiore! è l'April!
on-the fields-in flower! is the-April!
(to the fields in flower! it's April!)

Il piè trarrai fra mammole,
The foot will-go among violets,
(Feet will go among violets,)

avrai su'l petto rose e cilestrine,
you-will-have on-the breast roses and blues,
(you will have on your breast roses and blues,)

e le farfalle candide
and the butterflies pure
(and the pure butterflies)

t'aleggeranno intorno al nero crine.
you-they-flutter around to-the black hair.
(flutter around your black hair.)

Tosti
A Sera
At Evening

Bianca splende la luna, Voghiamo, o mio battel.
White shines the moon, They-row, o my boat.
(The moon shines white, Row, o my boat.)

Se il remo m'è fedel, voghiam!
If the oar me-is faithful, they-row!
(If the oar is faithful to me, row!)

Io rivedrò la mia diletta bruna, voghiam!
I will-see-again the my delight brown, they-row!
(I will see my brown-haired delight again, row!)

Della sua finestretta Veggo lontan sul mar
Of-the its little-window I-see far-away on-the sea
(From its little window I see far out to sea)

Il lume tremolar, voghiam!
The light trembles, they-row!
(The light trembles, row!)

Ella t'attende, o gondolier, t'affretta, Voghiam!
She you-awaits, o gondolier, you-it-hastens, They-row!
(She awaits you, o gondolier, it hastens you, row!)

O notte, quest'incanto Parla soave al cor
O night, this-enchantment Speaks sweet to-the heart
(O night, this enchantment speaks sweetly to the heart)

La canzone d'amor, voghiam!
The song of-love, they-row!
(the song of love, row!)

Ripeti o gondolier, disciogli il canto, voghiam!
You-repeat o gondolier, release the song, row!
(Repeat o gondolier, sing your song, row!)

Finchè vedrai billare Le stelle, io t'amerò,
Until you-will-see sparkle The stars, I you-will-love,
(Until you see the stars sparkle, I will love you,)

A te fedel sarò, voghiam!
To you faithful I-will-be, they-row!
(I will be faithful to you, row!)

Finchè la notte scenderà sul mare, Voghiam! Ah!
Until the night will-descend on-the sea, They-Row! Ah!
(Until the night descends on the sea, Row! Ah!)

Tosti
Ave Maria
Hail Mary

Per le fulgenti cupole dorate
For the shining domes bright
(From the shining bright domes,)

La melodia dell'organo suonava,
The melody of-the-organ will-sound,
(the organ melody will sound,)

Lento morira il dì sulle ventrate;
Slowly dies the day on-the sunsets;
(the day slowly dies on the sunsets;)

Una nube d'incenso al ciel volava,
A cloud of-incense to-the heaven will-fly,
(A cloud of incense will fly to heaven,)

E dolcemente da ogni labbro uscia: Ave Maria.
And sweetly of every lip emits: Hail Mary.
(And sweetly emits from every lip: Hail Mary.)

Nella blanda mestizia di quell'ora Tutta serenità di paradiso,
In-the bland sadness of that-hour All serenity of paradise,
(In the bland sadness of that hour All serenity of paradise,)

Il cavaliere che sospiro ognore M'apparve,
The cavalier that sighs always Me-appears,
(The cavalier who always sighs appears to me,)

e a lungo ci quardammo in viso:
and to long us they-look-at in face:
(and look at us in the face a long time:)

Fu vano al lora la preghiera mia, Ave Maria.
Was vain to-the their the prayer my, Hail Mary.
(My prayer to them was invain, Hail Mary.)

Dell'azzuro del ciel stendi la mano
Of-the-blue of-the heaven extends the hand
(From the blue of the heaven the hand extends)

A me infelice dal dolore affranta;
To me unhappy of-the sorrow exhausted;
(to my unhappy and exhausted sorrow;)

Deh! ch'io nel piano non t'invochi in vano,
Ah! that-I in-the tears not you-invoke in vain,
(Ah! that in tears I don't invoke you in vain,)

Arridi all'amor mio, Vergine santa:
You-smile to-the-love my, Virgin holy:
(You smile on my love, holy Virgin:)

Abbi pietà di me, Vergine pia, Ave Maria.
Have pity of me, Virgin pious, Hail Mary.
(Have pity on me, pious Virgin, Hail Mary.)

Tosti
'A Vucchella
A Little-Mouth

Sì comme'a nu sciorillo tu tiene na vucchella
Yes like-has a little-flower you have a little-mouth
(Yes, you have a little mouth like a little flower)

ne poco pocorillo appassuliatella.
a little bit passionate.
(a little bit passionate.)

Meh, dammillo,
Ah, give-me-it,
(Ah, give it to me,)

è comm'a na rusella damillo nu vasillo,
is like-to a little-brook give-me-it a little-kiss,
(like a little brook, give me a little kiss,)

dammillo, Cannetella! Dammillo e pigliatillo,
give-me-it, Cannetella! Give-me-it and take-you-one,
(give me it, Cannetella! give it to me and you take one,)

nu vaso piccerillo comm'a chesta vucchella,
a kiss so-long like-a this little-mouth,
(a long kiss like this little mouth,)

che pare na rusella nu poco pocorillo appassuliatella.
that like a little-brook a little bit passionate.
(that, like a little brook, is a little bit passionate.)

Sì tu tiene na vucchella ne poco pocorillo appassuliatella.
Yes you have a little-mouth a little bit passionate.
(Yes you have a little mouth which is a little bit passionate.)

Chanson de l'Adieu
Song of the-Farewell

Partir, c'est mourir un peu, C'est mourir a ce qu'on aime:
To-part, it's to-die a little, It's to-die to that which-one loves:
(To part, is to die a little, it's to die to that one which loves:)

On laisse un peu de soi-même
One loses a little of oneself
(One loses a little of oneself)

En toute heure et dans tout lieu.
In every hour and in every place.
(in every hour and in every place.)

C'est toujours le deuil d'un voeu, Le dernier vers d'un poème.
It's always the sorrow of-a vow, The last verse of-a poem.
(It's always the sorrow of a vow, The last verse of a poem.)

Et l'on part, et c'est un jeu, Et jusqu'à l'adieu suprême
And it-one parts, and it's a game, And until the-farewell last
(And one parts, and it's a game, And until the last farewell)

C'est son âme que l'on sème, en chaque adieu:
It's one's soul that it-one seems, in every farewell:
(It's one's soul that one seems, in every farewell:)

Partir, c'est mourir un peu.
To-part, it's to-die a little.
(To part, is to die a little.)

Tosti
Donna, Vorrei Morir
Lady, I-would-like To-die

Donna, vorrei morir, ma conforato
Lady, I-would-like to-die, but comforted
(Madame, I would like to die,)

Dall'onesto tuo amor;
of-the-honest your love;
(With your honest love, to be comforted;)

Sentirmi almeno una sol volta amato
Feel-me at-least a single time loved
(Without having blushed,)

Senza averne rossor.
Without having blushed.
(to feel loved at least once.)

Vorrei poterti dar quel po' che resta
I-would-like to-be-able-you to-give that little that stays
(I would like to be able to give you)

Della mia gioventù;
In-the my youth;
(that little bit still left of my youth;)

Sovra l'omero tuo piegar la testa
On the-shoulder your to-bend the head
(On your shoulder to bend my head)

E non destarmi più.
And not to-wake-up-me more.
(and no more to wake up.)

Dopo!
After!

Correa secura per le quete valli
She-ran steady in the quiet valleys
(She ran steady in the quiet valleys)

E di fiori campestri ornavo il crin;
And of flowers rustic adorned the hair;
(And rustic flowers adorned her hair;)

Ed un povero vezzo di coralli
And a poor necklace of coral
(And a poor coral necklace)

Faceva invidiato il mio destin
she-Made to-envy the my destiny
(she made to envy my destiny)

Ei venne un giorno; m'ingemmò la testa,
He came one day; me-I-will-bejewel the head,
(He came one day; I will bejewel my head,)

Di perle e di smeraldi ei mi coprì.
Of pearls and of emeralds they me cover.
(pearls and emeralds cover me.)

Fui regina la notte della festa,
Was queen the night of-the festival,
(She was queen the night of the festival,)

Fui derelitta quand sorge il dì.
Was abandoned when rose the day.
(she was abandoned when the day rose.)

Or se a caso l'incontro per le vie
Now if to house the-enchantment for the ways
(Now if the enchantment for the way of another woman)

Un'altra donna accanto gli sta,
Another woman beside him stays,
(stays beside him at home,)

Un'altra donna ch'ha le perle mie
Another woman who-she-has the pearls my
(Another woman who has my pearls,)

E che domani la mia sorte avrà.
And who tomorrow the my fate will-have.
(and who tomorrow will have my fate.)

Ed io pensando alle perdute valli,
And I thinking to-the lost valleys,
(And I, thinking of the lost valleys,)

Ai fior del campo che cogliea lassù,
To-the flowers of-the camp that gather up-there,
(to the flowers of the field that grow up there,)

Piango il povero vezzo di coralli,
I-weel the poor necklace of coral,
(I weep for the poor coral necklace,)

piango l'invidia che non desto più.
I-weep the-envy that not lively more.
(I weep for the envy which is lively no more.)

Ideale
Ideal

Io ti seguii come'iride di pace Lungo le vie del cielo;
I you follow like-irises of peace Long the ways of-the heaven;
(I follow you like irises of peace along the ways of heaven:)

Io ti seguii come un'amica face De la notte nel velo.
I you follow like a-friendly face Of the night in-the veil.
(I follow you like a friendly face in the darkness of night.)

E ti senti ne la luce, ne l'aria,
And you feel neither the light, nor the-air,
(And you feel neither the light, nor the air,)

Nel profumo dei fiori;
In-the perfume of-the flowers;
(In the perfume of the flowers;)

E fu piena la stanza solitaria Di te, dei tuoi splendori.
And was full the room solitary Of you, of-the your splendors.
(And with you the solitary room was full or your splendors.)

In te rapito, al suon de la tua voce
In you I-delight, at-the sound of the your voice
(I delight in you, I dreamed at great length)

Lungamente sognai,
At-great length I-dreamed,
(at the sound of your voice,)

E de la terra ogni affanno, ogni croce In quel giorno scordai.
And of the earth every pang, every cross In that day I-forgot.
(And every pang of the earth, In that day I forget every
cross.)

Torna, caro ideal, torna un istante A sorridermi ancora,
Return, dear ideal, return an instant To smile-me again,
(Return, dear ideal, return an instant to smile on me again,)

E a me risponderà nel tuo sembiante Una novell'aurora.
And to me will-shine in-the your appearance A new-dawn.
(And to me a new dawn will shine in your appearance.)

Torna, caro ideal, torna, torna.
Return, dear ideal, return, return.
(Return, dear ideal, return, return.)

Il pescatore canta!...
The fisherman sings!...

Hai le pupille così grandi e chiare che dentro a quelle
You-have the eyes so large and clear that within to those
(You have eyes so large and clear that within them)

si rispechia amore: O bella,
themselves reflect love: O beautiful-one,
(they reflect love: O beautiful one,)

che cammini lungo il mare,
that paths along the sea,
(on the paths along the sea,)

sovra la spiaggia canta un pescatore! Un pescatore canta
on the seashore sings the fisherman! A fisherman sings
(and on the seashore a fisherman sings! A fisherman sings)

e se me muore e tu cammini e non ti vuoi fermare:
and if me dies and you walk and not to-you wish to-stop:
(and if I die and you walk and you wish not to stop:)

Sorge la luna bianca come un fiore e il pecatore canta,
Rise the moon white like a flower and the fisherman sings,
(The moon rises white like a flower and the fisherman sings,)

e dorma il mare! O bella,
and sleeps the sea! O beautiful-one,
(and the sea sleeps! O beautiful one,)

il cuore mio tutto era d'oro
the heart my all was of-gold
(my heart was all golden)

e l'ho smarrito in una dolce sera;
and it-I-have lost in a sweet evening;
(and I have lost her in a sweet evening;)

v'erano tutte le sirene
you-they-are all the sirens
(to you they are all sirens)

in core ma chi la ritrovò, bella non c'era!
in heart but who her will-re-find, beautiful not of-it-was!
(in heart ah! who will find her again, beautiful it was not!)

E il pescatore canta: Amore, amore,
And the fisherman sings: Love, love,
(And the fisherman sings: Love, love,)

m'hai preso il cuore e non ti vuoi fermare!
me-you-have near the heart and not to-you wish to-stop!
(you I have near my heart and I don't wish to stop you!)

Invano!
Invain!

La serenata ch'io ti cantava era una lenta nenia d'amor;
The serenace that-I you sang was a slow wailing of-love;
(The serenade that I sang to you was a slow wailing of love;)

nei tristi accordi, io ti narvava tutto lo spasimo del mio dolor!
in-the sad chords, I you told all the agony of-the my sorrow!
(in the sad chords, I told you all the agony of my sorrow!)

Ma invan, tremando, la mia canzone
But invain, trembling, the my song
(But invain, trembling, like a lament)

come un lamento saliva al ciel;
like a lament ascended to-the heaven;
(my song ascended to heaven;)

tra' verdi rami del tuo balcone,
among-the green branches of-the your balcony,
(among the green branches of your balcony,)

tu sorridovi, bella e crudel!
you smile, beautiful and cruel-one!
(you smile, beautiful and cruel one!)

Or la romanza che ti ripeto
Now the romance that you repeat
(Now the romance that you repeat)

con altri accenti vola dal cor;
with other accents flies to-the heart;
(with other words flies to my heart;)

vibro nel ritmo fremente e lieto
vibrates in-the rhythm trembling and light
(vibrates in the trembling rhythm and a light)

una gioconda storia d'amor!
a happy story of-love!
(and happy love story!)

Ma invano echeggia la mia canzone
But invain resounds the my song
(But invain my song in a new joyful)

nel novo metro gaia e fedel:
in-the new meter joyful and faithful:
(and faithful meter resounds:)

tra i vezzi rami del tuo balcone tu non sorridi,
among the pretty branches of-the your balcony you not smile,
(among the pretty branches of your balcony you do not smile,)

bella e crudel! Ah! Ah!
beautiful and cruel-one! Ah! Ah!
(beautiful and cruel one! Ah! Ah!)

Io voglio amarti!
I wish to-love-you!

Come l'onda va il lido a bacciar,
Like the'wave goes the seashore to kiss,
(Like the wave goes to kiss the seashore,)

Come il sol manda raggi sul mar,
Like the sun sends rays on-the sea,
(Like the sun sends rays on the sea,)

Come un canto d'angel vola in alto nel ciel,
Like a song of-angel flies in high in-the heaven,
(Like an angel's song flies high in the heaven,)

così te ricordo, amor!
thus you I-remember, love!
(thus I remember you, love!)

Come il tralcio a la torre si tien,
Like the vine to the tower itself holds,
(Like the vine holds to the tower,)

come brina d'un fiore nel sen,
like dew of-a flower in-the breast,
(like dew in the breast of a flower,)

come l'ombra al fulgor e la notte all'albor,
like the-shadow to-the radiance and the night to-the-dawn,
(like the shadow to radiance and night to dawn,)

così a te avvinto ho in cor!
thus to you captivated I-have in heart!
(thus my heart is captivated with you!)

Come luna che fredda si sti su le nubi,
Like moon that cold itself stays on the clouds,
(Like the cold moon which stays on the clouds,)

o solinga senza, come roccia fatal,
oh lonely without, like rock fatal,
(oh without loneliness, like a fatal rock,)

che tentare non val, così tu non hai pietà!
that trying not value, thus you not have pity!
(that trying without success, thus you have no pity!)

Come l'alla notturna del gel
Like the-wing nightly of-the cold
(Like the nightly frost)

fa la rosa morir su lo stel,
makes the rose tò-die on the stem,
(that makes the rose die on the stem.)

come acuto pugnal squarcia un petto regal,
like sharp blow tears a breast regal,
(like a sharp blow tears a regal breast,)

così tu m'uccidi, o crudel!   Ma non vale
thus you me-kill, o cruel-one! But not value
(thus you kill me, o cruel one! But your blind severity)

il tuo cieco rigor, te pur vince un acceso dolor!
the your blind severity, you still win an enflamed sorrow!
(has no value, an enflamed sorrow you still win!)

Finchè in vita sarò, a te sempre dirò: Io t'amo!
Until in life will-be, to you always I-will-say: I you-love!
(Until your life will end, to you always I will say! I love you!)

Io t'amo, Io voglio amarti ognor!
I you-love, I wish to-love-you always!
(I love you, I want to love you always!)

L'alba separa dalla luce l'ombra
The-dawn separates from-the light the-shadow

L'alba separa dalla luce l'ombra
The-dawn separates from-the light the-shadow
(The dawn separates shadow from light)

e la mia voluttà dal mio desire.
and the my voluptousness from-the my desire.
(and my voluptousness from my desire.)

O dolci stelle, è l'ora di morire.
O sweet stars, is the-hour to die.
(O sweet stars, it's time to die.)

Un più divino amor dal ciel vi sgombra.
A more divine love from-the heaven you remove.
(A more divine love you remove from the heavens.)

Pupille ardenti, o voi senza ritorno stelle tristi,
Eyes ardent, oh you without return stars sad,
(Ardent eyes, oh you never returning sad stars,)

spegnetivi incorrotte!
die-out-you uncorrupted!
(you die out uncorrupted!)

Morir debbo. Veder non voglio io giorno,
To-die I-must. To-see not wish I day,
(I must die. I do not wish to see the day,)

per amor del mio sogno e della notte.
for love from-the my dream and from-the night.
(from my dream and from the night for love.)

Chiudimi, o Notte, nel tuo sen materno,
Hear-me, o Night, in-the your breast maternal,
(Hear me, o Night, in your maternal breast,)

mentre la terra pallida s'irrora.
while the earth pallid yourself-bedew.
(while the pallid earth bedews itself.)

Ma che dal sangue mio nasce l'aurora
But that of-the blood my births the-dawn
(But from my blood the dawn is born)

e dal sogno mio breve il sole eterno.
and from-the dream my brief the sun eternal.
(and from my brief dream the eternal sun.)

L'ultima canzone
The-last song

M'han detto che domani, Nina, vi fate sposa,
Me-they-have said that tomorrow, Nina, you make wife,
(They told me that tomorrow, Nina, you are getting married,)

ed io vi canto ancor la serenata!
and I you sing still the serenade!
(and I still serenade you!)

Là, nei deserti piani, là, ne la valle ombrosa,
There, in-the deserted plains, there, in the valleys shady,
(There, in the deserted plains, there, in the shady valleys,)

oh quante volte a voi l'ho ricantata!
oh how-many times to you it-I-have resung!
(oh how many times I sang it to you!)

"Foglia di rosa, o fiore d'amaranto, se ti fai sposa,
"Leaf of rose, o flower of-amaranth, if you make wife,
("Rose leaf, o amaranth flower, if you get married,)

io ti sto sempre accanto."
I you stay always beside."
(I will stay beside you always.")

Domani avrete intorno Feste sorrisi e fiori,
Tomorrow you-will-have around Festive smiles and flowers,
(Tomorrow you will have Festive smiles and flowers all
around,)

nè penserete ai nostri vecchi amori.
neither thinking to-the our old loves.
(neither thinking of our former loves.)

Ma sempre, notte e giorno, piena di passione
But always, night and day, full of passion,
(But always, night and day, full of passion,)

verrà gemendo a voi la mia canzone:
it-will-come moaning to you the my song:
(my song will come moaning to you:)

"Foglia di menta, o fiore di granato,
"Leaf of mint, o flower of deep-red,
("Mint leaf, o deep red flower,)

Nina, rammenta i baci che t'ho dato!"
Nina, recall the kisses that you-I-have given!"
(Nina, remember the kisses that I have given you!")

L'ultimo bacio
The-last kiss

Se tu lo vedi gli dirai che l'amo,
If you him see you-will-say that him-I-love,
(If you see him tell him that I love him,)

che l'amo ancora come ai primi dì,
that him-I-love still like to-the first days,
(that I still love him like in our first days,)

che nei languidi sogni ancor lo chiamo,
that in-the languid dreams still him I-call,
(that I still call to him in my languid dreams,)

lo chiamo ancor come se fosse qui.
him I-call still like if he-were here.
(I still call to him as if he were here.)

E gli dirai che colla fé tradita
And him you-will-say that with-the faith betrayed
(And you will tell him that with betrayed faith)

tutto il gaudio d'allor non mi rapì.
all the joy of-then not me stole.
(all the former joys he did not steal from me.)

E gli dirai che basta alla mia vita
And him you-will-say that enough to-the my life
(And you will tell him that enough to my life)

l'ultimo bacio che l'addio finì.
the-last kiss that the-farewell I-ended.
(was the last kiss that ended our farewell.)

Nessun lo toglie dalla bocca mia
No one it removes from-the mouth my
(No one removed from my mouth)

l'ultimo bacio che l'addio finì.
the-last kiss that the-farewell I-ended.
(the last kiss that ended our farewell.)

Ma se vuoi dargli un altro
But if you-wish to-give-him an other
(But if you wish to give him another,)

in compagnia digli che l'amo,
in company tell-him that him-I-love,
(tell him that I love him,)

e che l'aspetto qui.
and that him-I-await here.
(and that I await him here.)

Lamento d'amore
Lament of-love

Perché ti deggio amar d'amor sì tanto,
Why you I-must to-love of-love so much,
(Why must I love you with so much love,)

Se tu non m'ami dell'istesso amor?
If you not me-love of-the-same love?
(If you do not love me with the same love?)

Forse il destin che mi dannava al pianto, ah,
Perhaps the destiny that me condemned to-the crying, ah,
(Perhaps the destiny that condemned me to crying, ah,)

come croce l'impose a quest cor.
like cross it-imposes to this heart.
(like a cross imposes itself on this heart.)

Ma forse il di verrà che m'amerai pentita
But perhaps the day will-come that me-you-will-love
repentant
(But perhaps the day will come that you will love me)

di mostrarti a me crudel.
to show-you to me cruel-one.
(and show me your repentance, cruel one.)

Ma sarà tardi, e invan mi chiamerai,
But you-will-be late, and invain me you-will-call,
(But you will be late, and invain you will call me,)

che sceso sarò già nel freddo avel.
that gone I-will-be already in-the cold tomb.
(I will already be gone into the cold tomb.)

E allora che una mesta e pia preghiera,
An then that a sad and pious prayer,
(And then from your lips a sad and pious prayer)

dal labbro tuo farai a Dio salir?
of-the lip you will-make to God to-rise?
(will rise to God?)

Sovra l'ali dell'aure della sera,
On the-wings of-the-breezes of-the evening,
(Send your sigh to my tomb,)

Alla mia tomba manda un tuo sospir,
To-the my tomb send a your sigh,
(on the wings of the evening breezes,)

E se sull'imbrunire in veste nera,
And if on-the-darkness in vest black,
(And if in the black vest of darkness,)

visiterai di morte la città,
you-will-visit of death the city,
(you will visit the city of death,)

vedrai sulla mio fossa errar leggera
you-will-see on-the my grave wandering lightly
(you will see on my grave wandering lightly)

una fiammella che ti seguirà.
a brightness that you will-follow.
(a brightness that you will follow.)

Sarà l'ultimo fremito d'amore
You-will-be the-last shiver of-love
(You will feel again my last sign,)

che il cenno mio per te risentirà.
that the sign my for you it-will-feel-again.
(you will be my last shiver of love.)

Della fiammella il tremulo bagliore
Of-the brightness the tremulant gleam
(The tremulant gleam of brightness will tell)

come e quanto t'amai ti narrerà,
how and how-much you-I-loved you it-will-tell,
(how and how much I loved you,)

dal freddo avel ti narrerà,
of-the cold tomb you it-will-tell,
(The cold tomb will tell you)

come e quanto t'amai ti narrerà.
how and how-much you-loved you it-will-tell.
(how and how much I loved you.)

Tosti
La mia canzone!
The my song!

La mia canzone è un dolce mormoria
The my song is a sweet murmur
(My song is a sweet murmur)

Che sino a te, nell'aria fredda, sale;
That until to you, in-the-air cold, strengthens;
(that to you, in the cold air, strengthens;)

E, se ti parla ancor dell'amor mio,
And, if to-you it-speak still of-the-love my,
(And, if it still speaks to you of my love,)

Cara fanciulla, non ti vuol far male,
Dear young-girl, not you want to-make harm,
(Dear young girl, I do not wish you harm,)

Vagando sul tuo candido guanciale,
Wandering on-the your pure pillow,
(Wandering on your pure pillow,)

Essa vuol dirti un ultimo desio:
She wants to-tell-you a last desire:
(She wants to tell you her last wish:)

Su la tua bianca fronte verginale.
On the your white forehead virginal.
(On your white virginal forehead.)

La mia canzone è il bacio dell'addio.
The my song is the kiss of-the-farewell.
(My song is the kiss of farewell.)

La mia canzone sospirando muore
The my song sighing dies
(My sighing song dies)

Lieve nell'aria su la tua vetrata;
Light in-the-air on the your window;
(lightly in the air on your window;)

Ma, disfidando il gelo e il tenebrore,
But, defying the cold and the darkness,
(But, defying the cold and darkness,)

Reca il desio d'un'anima agitata;
It-brings the desire of-a-soul agitated;
(it brings my soul's agitated desire;)

E vuol destar ogn'ansia a te più grata,
And you-wish to-awake every-anxiety to you more pleasant,
(And you wish to awaken every more pleasant anxiety,)

Ogni affetto sopito entro il tuo core:
Every affection soothed within the your heart:
(every soothed affection within your heart:)

Ora che tu sei sola, addormentata,
Now that you are alone, asleep,
(Now that you are alone, asleep,)

La mia canzone è un fremito d'amore!
The my song is a shiver of-love!
(My song is a shiver of love!)

Tosti
La Serenata
The Serenade

Vola, o serenata: La mia diletta è sola,
Fly, o serenade: The my delight is alone,
(Fly, o serenade: My delight is alone,)

e, con la bella testa abbandonata,
and, with the beautiful head abandoned,
(and, with her beautiful abandoned head,)

posa tra le lenzuola: O serenata, vola.
place among the sheets: O serenade, fly.
(fly between her sheets: O serenade, fly.)

Splende pura la luna, l'ale il silenzio stende,
Shines clear the moon, the-wings the silence extend,
(The moon shines brightly, silence extends its wings,)

e dietro i veni dell'alcova bruna
and behind the veils of-the-alcove brown
(and behind the shadows of the brown alcove)

la lampada s'accende. Pura la luna splende.
the lamp itself-burns. Clear the moon shines.
(the lamp burns. The moon shines brightly.)

Vola, o serenata, vola. Ah! là. Ah! là.
Fly, o serenade, fly. Ah! there. Ah! there.
(Fly, o serenade, fly. Ah! there. Ah! there.)

Vola, o serenata: La mia diletta è sola;
Fly, o serenade: The my delight is alone;
(Fly, o serenade: My delight is alone;)

ma, sorridendo ancor mezzo assonnata, torna fra le lenzuola: but,
smiling still half sounded, return among the sheets:
(but, still smiling half muted, return between her sheets:)

O serenata, vola.
O serenade, fly.
(O serenade, fly.)

L'onda sogna su 'l lido, e 'l vento su la fronda;
The-wave dreams on the shore, and the wind on the branch;
(The wave dreams on the shore, and the wind on the branch;)

e a' baci miei ricusa ancora un nido la mia signora bionda.
and to-the kisses my denies still a nest the my lady blonde.
(and my blonde lady still denies a place for my kisses.)

Sogna su 'l lido l'onda.
Dreams on the shore the-wave.
(The wave dreams on the shore.)

Vola, o serenata, vola. Ah! là.
Fly, o serenade, fly. Ah! there.
(Fly, o serenade, fly. Ah! there.)

Tosti
Luna d'estate!...
Moon of-summer!...

Luna d'estate, ho un sogno nel mio cuore
Moon of-summer, I-have a dream in-the my heart
(Summer moon, I have a dream in my heart)

e vo' cantando tutta notte al mare:
and I-wish singing all night to-the sea:
(and I want to sing all night to the sea:)

mi son fermato a una finestra in fiore,
me am stopped at a window in flower,
(I am stopped at an open window,)

perché l'anima mia febbre ha d'amore.
because the-soul my excitement it-has of-love.
(because my soul has the excitement of love.)

Mi son fermato a una finestra in fiore
Me am stopped at a window in flower
(I am stopped at an open window)

ove son due pupille affatturate.
where are two eyes bewitched.
(where two eyes are bewitched.)

E chi le guarda soffre per amore e sogna per desio,
And who them sees suffers for love and dreams of desire,
(And he who sees them suffers for love and dreams of desire,)

luna d'estate! Luna d'estate, amore è come il mare
moon of-summer! Moon of-summer, love is like the sea
(summer moon! Summer moon, love is like the sea)

ed il mio cuore è un'onda senza posa:
and the my heart is a-wave without rest:
(and my heart is a wave without rest:)

ma solamente lo potran fermare le pupille
but only it will-be-able to-stop the eyes
(but only it will be able to stop your eyes)

e il labbro suo di rosa.
and the lip your of red.
(and your red lips.)

E vo' cantando tutta notte al mare
And I-wish singing all night to-the sea
(And I want to sing all night to the sea)

per quelle due pupille addormentate.
of those two eyes adored.
(of those two adored eyes.)

Ho il pianto agli occhi e la speransa in cuore
I-have the crying to-the eyes and the hope in heart
(I have tears in my eyes and hope in my heart)

e splendo come te,
and I-shine like you,
(and I shine like you,)

luna d'estate!
moon of-summer!
(summer moon!)

Lungi
Far-away

Lungi, sull'ali del canto
Far-away, on-the-wings of-the song
(Far away, on the song's wings)

di qui lungi recare io ti vo'.
of here far-away to-bring I you wish.
(I wish to bring you here from afar.)

Là, nei campi fioriti del santo Gange,
There, in-the fields flowered of-the holy Ganges,
(There, in the flowered fields of the holy Ganges,)

un luogo bellissimo io so.
a place very-beautiful I know.
(I know a very beautiful place.)

Ivi rosso un giardino risplende
In-that-place red a garden to-shine
(In that red place in quiet glimmer)

della luna nel cheto chiaror:
of-the moon in-the quiet glimmer:
(the moon shines on the garden:)

ivi il fiore del loto ti attende,
in-that-place the flower of-the lotus you it-awaits,
(in that place the lotus flower awaits you,)

o soave sorella dei fior.
o sweet sister of-the flower.
(o sweet sister of the flower.)

Le viole bisbiglian vezzose,
The violets whisper pretty,
(Sweetly the violets whisper,)

guardan gli astri su alto passar;
they-look-at the stars on high passing;
(they look at the stars passing on high;)

e fra loro si chinan le rose odorose novelle a cantar.
and among them one bends the roses fragrant new to sing.
(and among them one bends the fragrant roses to sing anew.)

Oh, che sensi d'amore di calma,
how you-feel of-love of calm,
(Oh, how you feel the calm of love,)

beveremo nell'aure colà! Oh,
we-will-drink in-the-breezes there!
(we will drink there in the breezes!)

Sogneremo, seduti a una palma,
We-will-dream, charmed at a palm,
(We will dream, charmed at a palm tree,)

lunghi sogni di felicità.
long dreams of happiness.
(long dreams of happiness.)

Tosti
Malìa
Charm

Cosa c'era ne 'l fior che m'hai dato?
Thing that-was of-it the flower that me-you-have given?
(Was it a flower that you gave me?)

Forse un filtro, un arcano poter!
Perharps a love-potion, a mystery might-be!
(Perhaps a love potion, maybe a mystery!)

Ne 'l toccarlo, 'l mio core ha tremato,
Of-it the to-touch-it, the my heart has trembled,
(To touch it, my heart trembled,)

m'ha l'olezzo turbato 'l pensier!
me-you-have the-fragrance troubled the thought!
(the fragrance you have given me troubled my thought!)

Ne le vaghe movenze che ci hai?
Of-it the pretty movements that here you-have?
(Here do you have pretty movements?)

Un incanto vien forse con te?
An enchantment comes perhaps with you?
(Perhaps an enchantment comes with you?)

Freme l'aria per dove tu vai,
Trembles the-air for where you go,
(Where you go the air trembles,)

spunta un fiore ove passa 'l tuo piè!
rises a flower where passes the your foot!
(a flower rises where your foot passes!)

Io non chiedo qual plaga beata fina adesso soggiorno ti fu;
I not ask which country blessed fine now sojurn to-you was;
(I do not ask which blessed fine country you came from;)

non ti chiedo se ninfa, se fata,
not you I-ask if nymph, if fairy,
(I do not ask if you are a nymph,)

se una bionda parvenza sei tu!
if a blonde appearance are you!
(a fairy, a blonde vision!)

Ma che c'è ne 'l tuo sguardo fatale?
But that that-is of-it the your glance fatal?
(But is your glance fatal?)

Cosa ci hai ne 'l tuo magico dir?
Thing here you-have of-it the your magic to-say?
(Have you here something magic to say?)

Se mi guardi, un'ebbrezza m'assale,
If me you-see, an-elation me-assails,
(If you see me, I am elated,)

se mi parli, mi sento morir!
if to-me you-speak, me I-feel to-die.
(if you speak to me, I feel like dying.)

Tosti
Marechiare
(Sea-bright)

Quando sorge la luna a Marechiare,
When rises the moon to Sea-bright,
(When the moon rises on Marechiare,)

perfino i pesci tremano d'amore,
even the fish tremble of-love,
(even the fish tremble with love,)

si sconvolgono l'onde in grembo al mare,
one turns-upside-down the-waves in bosom to-the sea,
(the wave turns upside down in the bosom of the sea,)

e per la gioia cangiano colore.
and for the joy they-change color.
(and for joy they-change color.)

A Marechiare sorride un balcone,
To Marechiare smiles a balcony,
(A balcony smiles to Marechiare,)

la passione mia vi batte l'ale:
the passion my to-you beats the-wings:
(my passion beats its wings to you:)

l'acqua canta di sotto una canzone,
the-water sings of quiet a song,
(the water softly sings a song,)

un garofano olezze al davanzale.
a clove frangrances to-the window-sill.
(a clove perfumes the window sill.)

Chi dice che le stelle son lucenti,
Who says that the stars are bright,
(Who says that the stars are bright,)

degli occhi tuoi non vide lo splendore!
of-the eyes your not it-sees the splendor!
(it does not see the splendor of your eyes!)

Li conosco io ben quei raggi ardenti!
Them know I well those rays ardent!
(I know well those ardent rays!)

Ne scendono le punte in questo core!
Of-it the-descend the pains in this heart!
(From it they descend their pains on this heart!)

Destati, che la sera è tutto incanto,
Awake, that the evening is all enchanted,
(Awake, the evening is all enchanted,)

e mai per tanto tempo io t'ho aspettata!
and never for all time I you-have awaited!
(and I have awaited you for all time!)

Per accoppiar gli accordi al mesto canto,
To join the chords to-the sad song,
(To join my chords to the sad song,)

stasera una chitarra ho qui portata!
this-evening a guitar I-have here brought!
(I have brought a guitar here!)

Tosti
Mattinata
Morning

Mary, tremando l'ultima stella
Mary, trembling the-last star
(Mary, the trembling last star)

Nel vasto azzuro Tra poco vanirà;
In-the vast blue Among little will-fade;
(will fade in the vast blue sky;)

E presso a sorgere l'alba novella,
Is near to rise the-dawn new,
(The new dawn is close to rising,)

Con un susurro L'aura l'annunzia già.
With a whisper The-breeze the-announcement already.
(Already the breeze whispers the announcement.)

Io non ti dico, vieni al verone;
I not to-you speak, come to-the balcony;
(I dare not speak to you, come to the balcony;)

Mary, in quest'ore Più dolce è riposar;
Mary, in these-hours More sweet is to-rest;
(Mary, it is sweeter to rest in these hours;)

Mormoro basso la mia canzone,
Murmur low the my song,
(My song murmurs softly,)

Che il tuo sopore Non giunga ad abbreviar...
That the your lethargy Not arrives to shorten...
(that your lethargy does not come to shorten...)

Solo domando, solo desio
Only I-ask, only I-desire
(I only ask, I only desire)

Che il canto mio Lambendo il tuo guancial,
That the song my Skimming the your forehead,
(that my song skimming your forehead,)

Versi, o fanciulla, nella tuo mente
Pour-out, o little-girl, in-the your mind
(Pour out, o little girl, the bright wave in your mind,)

L'onda lucente D'un sogno celestial!
The-wave bright, Of-a dream heavenly!
(of a heavenly dream!)

Tosti
Nella notte d'avril
In-the night of'April

Nella notte d'avril, vien come un mite susurro
In-the night of-April, come like a mild whisper
(In an April night, come like a mild whisper)

da le siepi rifiorite la canzone d'amore:
to the hedges flourishing the song of-love:
(to the flourishing hedges the song of love:)

Pare un sospiro, un fremito, un desio;
Like a sigh, a shiver, a desire;
(Like a sigh, a shiver, a desire;)

ed or è un lungo bacio, or un addio che lentament muore.
and now is a long kiss, now a farewell what slowly dies.
(and it's now a long kiss, now a farewell that slowly dies.)

Dice la luna al fior: La notte è bella!
Says the moon to-the flower: The night is beautiful!
(The moon says to the flower: The night is beautiful!)

Dicon le rose: A le più vaghe anela,
Say the roses: To the most lovely it-gasps,
(The roses say: To the most lovely is gasps,)

Noi formerem corone! Sospira il vento:
We will-form crown! Sighs the wind:
(We will form a crown! The wind sighs:)

Oh che profumi! e poi, nella notte d'april,
Oh what perfumes! and then, in-the night of-April
(Oh what perfumes! and then, in an April night,)

ripete a voi la tenera canzone.
repeats to you the tender song.
(repeats the tender song to you.)

Ninna, nanna, nio figliolo!
Lullaby, my son!

Ninna nanna, mio figliolo! Ninna nanna, occhi ridenti!
Lullaby, my son! Lullaby, eyes smiling!
(Go to sleep, my son! Go to sleep, smiling eyes!)

Canta, canta, rosignolo, che il mio bimbo s'addormenti!
Sing, sing, nightingale, that the my baby he-slumbers!
(Sing, sing nightingale, so that my baby falls asleep!)

Fresche rose, gigli aulenti, ne la culla è il mio figliolo.
Fresh roses, lilies fragrant, in the cradle is the my son.
(Fresh roses, fragrant lilies, my son is in the cradle.)

Ninna nanna! Le lenzuola son tessute di contento.
Lullaby! The sheets are woven of contentment.
(Go to sleep! The sheets are woven with contentment.)

Oro fino era la spola ed i licci erano argento;
Gold fine was the shuttle and the heddles were silver;
(Fine gold was the shuttle and the heddles were silver;)

e pareva un istrumento quel telaio, una viola!
and it-seemed an implement that loom, a violet!
(That loom seemed like an implement, a violet!)

Benedetto! Non c'è duolo pel mio bimbo, non tormento.
Blessed! Not it-is sorrow for-the my baby, not torment.
(Be blessed! My baby has no sorrow, no torment.)

Ninna nanna! Il suo lenzuolo è tessuto di contento.
Lullaby! The his sheet is woven of contentment.
(Go to sleep! His sheet is woven with contentment.)

Ninna nanna! Il lume è spento, ma riluce il mio figliolo.
Lullaby! The light is exhausted, but shines the my son.
(Go to sleep! The light is out, but my son shines.)

Ninna nanna.
Lullaby.
(Go to sleep.)

Tosti
Ninon
Ninon

Ninon, Ninon, que fais-tu de la vie?
Ninon, Ninon, what make-you of the life?
(Ninon, Ninon, what are your doing with your life?)

L'heure s'enfuit, le jour succède au jour.
The-hour it-flees, the day follows to-the day.
(The hours fly, day follows day.)

Rose ce soir, demain flétrie.
Pink this night, tomorrow withered.
(Tonight is pink, tomorrow it's withered.)

Comment vis-tu, toi qui n'as pas d'amour?
How say-you, you who not-has not of-love?
(What do you say, you who knows not love?)

Ninon, demain l'hiver. Aujourd'hui le printemps,
Ninon, tomorrow the-winter. Today the spring,
(Ninon, tomorrow is winter. Today is spring,)

Quoi! tu n'as pas d'étoile, et tu vas sur la mer!
What! you not-have not of-star, and you go on the sea!
(What! you don't have a star, and you go to sea!)

Au combat sans musique, en voyage sans livre!
To-the combat without music, in voyage without journal!
(To combat without music, in voyage without journal!)

Quoi! tu n'as pas d'amour, et tu parles de vivre!
What! you not-have not of-love, and you speak of living!
(What! you do not have love, and you speak of living!)

Moi, pour un peu d'amour je donnerais mes jours;
Me, for a little of-love I will-give my days;
(Me, for a little love I will give my days;)

et je les donnerais pour rien sans les amours.
and I them will-give for nothing without the loves.
(and I will give nothing for days without love.)

Qu'importe que le jour finisse et recommence,
What-import that the day ends and re-begins,
(What importance has the day's end and rebeginning,)

quand d'une autre existence le coeur est animé?
when of-an other existence the heart is animated?
(When the heart is animated with another existence?)

Ouvrez-vous, jeunes fleurs; si la mort vous enlève,
Open-you, young flowers; if the death you raise,
(Open, young flowers; it you raise death,)

la vie est un sommeil, l'amour en est le rêve,
the life is a slumber, the love it is the dream,
(life is slumber, love is a dream,)

et vous aurez vécu, si vous avez aimé.
and you will-have lived, if you have loved.
(and you will have lived, if you have loved.)

Tosti
Non t'amo più!
Not you-I-love more!

Ricordi ancora il dì che c'incontrammo;
Remember still the day that we-met;
(Do you still remember the day we met;)

le tue promesse le ricordi ancor?
the your promises the you-remember still?
(do you still remember your promises?)

Folle d'amore io ti seguii, ci amammo,
Folly of-love I you followed, we loved,
(Madly in love, I followed you, we loved,)

e accanto a te sognai, folle d'amor.
and near to you I-dreamed, folly of-love.
(and near to you I dreamed, madly in love.)

Sogna, felice, di carezze
I-dreamed, happy, of caresses
(I dreamed, happy, a chain of caresses)

e baci una catena dileguante in ciel.
and kisses a chain disappeared in heaven.
(and kisses disappeared in heaven.)

Ma le parole tue furon mandaci,
But the words your fury lies,
(My fury lies in your words,)

perché l'anima tua fatta è di gel.
because the-soul your made is of cold.
(because your soul is made of ice.)

Te ne ricordi ancor, te ne ricordi ancor?
You of-it remember still, you of-it remember still?
(Do you still remember it, do you still remember it?)

Or la mia fede, il desiderio immenso,
Now the my faith, the desire immense,
(Now my faith, my immense desire,)

il mio sogno d'amor non sei più tu:
the my dream of-love not are more you:
(no more are you my dream of love:)

I tuoi baci non cerco, a te non penso;
The your kisses not I-find, to you not I-think;
(I cannot find your kisses; I do not think of you;)

sogno un altro ideal; non t'amo più.
I-dream an other ideal; not you-I-love more.
(I dream of another ideal; no more do I love you.)

Nei cari giorni che passamo insieme,
In-the dear days that we-passed together,
(In the dear days that we passed together,)

io cosparsi di fiori il tuo sentier.
I scattered of flowers the your path.
(I scattered your path with flowers.)

Tu fosti del mio cor l'unica speme,
You were of-the my heart the-only hope,
(You were the only hope of my heart,)

tu della mente l'unico pensier.
you of-the mind the-only thought.
(you the only thought of my mind.)

Tu m'hai visto pregare, impallidire,
You me-have seen praying, becoming-pale,
(You have seen my praying, turning pale,)

piangere tu m'hai visto innanzi a te.
crying you me-have seen before to you.
(you have seen me crying before you.)

Io sol per appagare un tuo desire avrei dato
I alone to satisfy a your desire I-have given
(To satisfy your desire I alone have given)

il mio sangue e la mia fé.
the my blood and the my faith.
(my blood and my faith.)

Penso!
I-think!

Penso alla prima volta in cui volgesti lo sguardo tuo
I-think to-the first time in whom you-turned the glance your
(I think of the first time you turned your sweet glance)

soave insino a me, ai dolce incanto,
sweet till to me, to-the sweet enchantment,
(toward me, to the sweet enchantment,)

ai palpiti celesti
to-the palpitations celestial
(to the celestial palpitations)

che quell'instante tenero mi diè.
that that-instant tender me gave.
(that that tender instant gave me.)

Ma tu...tu l'hai scordato, dici che un sogno fu.
But you...you it-have forgotten, you-say that a dream was.
(But you...you have forgotten it, you say that it was a dream.)

Come in quel dì beato
Like in that day blessed
(Like in that blessed day)

non sai guardami più.
not you-know to-look-at-me more.
(when you no longer knew how to look at me.)

Penso al sorriso che mirai primiero
I-think to-the smile that I-looked first
(I think of the very sweet smile on your lips)

sul labbro tuo
on-the lips your
(to which my eyes wandered)

dolcissimo vagar, alle speranze, al sogno lusinghiero
very-sweetly to-wander, to-the hopes, to-the dream favorable
(to hopes, to the favorable dream)

Penso!
(cont.)

che mi seppe nell'animo destar.
that me it-knew in-the-soul to-stir.
(that my soul knew to be excited.)

Ma tu...tu l'hai scordato, dici che un sogno fu.
But you...you it-have forgotten, you-say that a dream was.
(But you...you have forgotten it, you say it was a dream.)

Come in quel dì beato non sai sorrider più.
Like in that day blessed not you-know to-smile more.
(Like in that blessed day you no longer knew how to smile.)

Pour un baiser
For a kiss

Pour un baiser sur ta peau parfumée,
For a kiss on your skin fragrant,
(For a kiss on your fragrant skin,)

pour un baiser dans l'or de tes cheveux,
for a kiss on the-gold of your hair,
(for a kiss on your blond hair,)

reçois mon âme toute, ô bienaimée!
receive my soul all, o well-beloved!
(receive all my soul, o beloved!)

Tu comblerais l'infini de mes voeux par un baiser.
You would-fulfill the-infinity of my vows by a kiss.
(You would fulfill the infinite desire of my vows by a kiss.)

Pour un baiser distillé dans tes lévres, profond,
For a kiss dropped on your lips, profound,
(For a kiss placed on your lips, profound,)

tenace et lent comme un adien, souffrir le mal d'amour
held and slowly like a farewell, to-suffer the evil of-love
(held and slowly, like a farewell, to suffer the evil of love)

et de ses fièvres brûler,
and of those fevers to-burn,
(and burn of those fevers,)

languir et mourir peu à peu dans un baiser.
to-languish and to-die little by little in a kiss.
(to languish and to die little by little in a kiss.)

Tosti
Preghiera
Prayer

Alla mente confusa di dubbio e di dolore soccorri,
To-the mind confused of doubt and of sorrow you-held,
(Confused with doubt and sorrow, you held my mind,)

o mio Signore,
o my Lord,
(o my Lord,)

Col raggio dell fé sollevala dal peso
With-the ray of-the faith you-raise-it of-the weight
(with a ray of faith you lift the weight)

che la declina al fango: A te sospiro e piango,
that it sinks to-the mire: To you I-sigh and I-cry,
(that sinks me into the mire: To you I sigh and I cry,)

mi raccomando a te.
me entrusting to you.
(entrusting myself to you.)

Sai che la vita mia si strugge a poco a poco,
You-know that the life my itself struggles a little by little,
(You know that my life itself struggles little by little,)

come la cera al foco, come la neve al sol.
like the wax to-the fire, like the snow to-the sun.
(like wax to the fire, like snow to the sun.)

All'anima che anela di ricovrarti in braccio, deh!
To-the-soul that pants of taking-refuge-you in arm, ah!
(To the soul that gasps at taking refuge in your arms, ah!)

rompi, Signore, il laccio che le impedesce il vol.
break, Lord, the string that them impedes the flight.
(break, Lord, the string that impedes their flight.)

Signor, pietà!
Lord, pity!
(Lord, have pity!)

Primavera
Spring

Lungo i cheti sentieri il biancospin verdeggia;
Along the quiet paths the hawthorn green;
(Along the quiet paths of green hawthorn;)

dai fiorenti verzieri la primavera cochieggia.
from-the blooming gardens the spring it-appears.
(from the blooming gardens spring appears.)

Vuoi tu meco fuggir? Vuoi tu meco venir?
Wish you me-with to-flee? Wish you me-with to-come?
(Do you want to flee with me? Do you wish to come with me?)

Bimba da gl'occhi neri, lungo i cheti sentieri?
Baby of the-eyes black, along the quiet paths?
(Baby with black eyes, along the quiet paths?)

Sotto i soli fulgenti la selve ecco si desta;
Under the suns shining the shade there-is itself awakened;
(Under the shining suns the shade is awakened;)

e all'aure rinascenti amor confida in festa.   and to-the-breezes
reborn love it-confides in rejoicing.
(and to the breezes reborn love confides its rejoicing.)

Vuoi tu meco fuggir? Vuoi tu meco venir?
Wish you me-with to-flee? Wish you me-with to-come?
(Do you want to flee with me? Do you want to come with me?)

Bimba da gli occhi ardenti, sotto i soli fulgenti?
Baby of the eyes ardent, under the suns shining?
(Baby with ardent eyes, under the shining suns?)

Tosti
Ricordati di me
Remember-you of me

Non mancarmi d'amor, non darmi obblio,
Not to-lack-me of-love, not to-give-me oblivion,
(Don't deprive me of love, don't let me forget,)

ch'io son lontano e vivo sempre solo;
that-I am far-away and I-live always alone;
(that I am far away and I live always alone;)

come un fior tra le spine è il core mio,
like a flower among the thorns is the heart my,
(my heart is like a flower among thorns,)

pieno e dolce di affetti in mezzo al duolo.
full and sweet of affections in midst to-the sorrow.
(sweet and full of affections in the midst of sorrow.)

Non obbliarmi! e quando il sol declina sui nostri monti,
Not forget-me! and when the sun sets on-the your mountains,
(Don't forget me! and when the sun sets on your mountains,)

e i campi si fan mesti, ricordati di me,
and the fields they make sad, remember-you of me,
(and they make the fields sad, remember me,)

di la divina nota d'amor che, lieta, mi dicesti.
of the divine note of-love that, happy, me I-told-you.
(of the divine love note that, happy I told you.)

La tua gentil sembianza ò sempre in petto, lo guardo,
The your gentle image I-have always in breast, it I-see,
(Your gentle image I have always in my breast, I see it,)

i vezzi, i palpiti, i sospiri;
the habits, the palpitations, the sighs;
(the customs, the palpitations, the sighs;)

nel cor mi porterò l'antico affetto,
in-the heart me I-will-bring the-old affection,
(I will bring the former affections to my heart,)

fiorirò la mia speme coi desiri.
will-flower the my hopes with-the desires.
(my hopes will flower with desires.)

Non obbliarmi, o caro angiol d'amore;
Not forget-me, o dear angel of-love;
(Don't forget me, o dear angel of love;)

Rammentati di me che t'amo tanto;
Remember-you of me that you-I-love so-much;
(Of me remember that I love you very much;)

serbami sempre la tua fede in core,
keep-me always the your faith in heart,
(I always keep your faith in my heart,)

che non tramonti questo arcano incanto!
that not disappears this mysterious enchantment!
(that this mysterious enchantment doesn't disappear!)

Tosti
Ridonami la calma!
Re-give-me the calm!

Ave Maria, per l'aria va il suon d'una campana.
Hail Mary, on the-air goes the sound of-a bell.
(Hail Mary, the sound of the bell travels on the air.)

Sorge Venere pura e solitaria da la selva lontana.
Shines Venus pure and solitary on the forest far-away.
(On the far away forest pure and solitary Venus shines.)

Oh! come si diffonde del vespero la pace!
Oh! like one spreads of-the evening the peace!
(Oh! like peace spreads itself in the evening!)

La rondine ritorna a le sue gronde
The swallow returns to the his eaves
(The swallow returns to his eaves)

e là s'addorme e tace.
and there himself-falls-asleep and is-silent.
(and there falls asleep and is silent.)

Resta un murmure lento di mille voci strane.
Rests a murmur slow of 1000 voices odd.
(Of 1000 odd voices a slow murmur rests.)

Forse tra i fiori e tra le siepi
Perhaps among the flowers and among the hedges
(Perhaps among flowers and among hedges)

il vento racconta storie arcane.
the wind retells stories mysterious.
(the wind tells again the mysterious stories.)

Chi sa quanti pensieri in quel susurro grato!
Who knows how-many thoughts in that whisper pleasant! (Who knows all the thoughts in that pleasant whisper!)

Il vento canta e sopra i cimiteri
The wind sings and on the cemeteries
(The wind sings and passes on the cemeteries)

e i giardini è passato.
and the gardens is passed.
(and the gardens.)

Ave Maria, nel core comm'è dolce la sera?
Hail Mary, in-the heart like-is sweet the night?
(Hail Mary, is the night sweet like in my heart?)

Tu sai che ne' tormenti
You know that in-the torments
(You know that in the torments)

dell'amore è schietta la preghiera;
of-the-love is sincere the prayer;
(of love prayer is sincere;)

ond'io, nel cielo fiso lo sguardo umido e l'alma:
whence-I, in-the heaven fix the glance moist and the-soul:
(whence I, in heaven fix a moist glance and the soul:)

"Ridonami, ti prego, il mio sorriso;
"Re-give-me, you I-pray, the my smile;
("Return to me, I pray you, my smile;)

Ridonami la calma!"
Re-give-me the calm!"
(Return to me calm!")

Tosti
Rosa
Rose

Una povera rosa è rinserrata
A poor rose is closed
(A poor rose is closed)

nel tuo piccolo libro di preghiera,
in-the your small book of prayer,
(in your small prayer book,)

una povera rosa di brughiera,
a poor rose of moor,
(a poor rose from the moor,)

che la lunga stagione ha disseccata.
that the long season has parched.
(that the long season has parched.)

Chi te l'ha dato quel mesto fiore?
Who you it-has given that sad flower?
(Who has given you that sad flower?)

Qual ti rammenta sogno gentil?
What you recall dream gentle?
(Do you recall such a gentle dream?)

Ah! tu rispondi: Fugge l'amore!
Ah! you respond: Flee the-love!
(Ah! you respond: love flees!)

fuggon le splendide sere d'april!
we-flee the splendid evenings of April!
(we flee from the splendid April evenings!)

Or muta la contempli e d'improvviso,
Now mute she you-behold and of-sudden,
(Suddenly you behold her now mute,)

ti si vela di pianto la pupilla:
you yourself veil of tears the eye:
(tears veil your eyes:)

or, la baci, tremando, e disfavilla,
now, the kiss, trembling, and it-sparkles,
(now, the kiss, trembling, and sparkles,)

su la tua fronte, un vivido sorriso!
on the your face, a vivid smile!
(on your face, a vivid smile!)

Segreto
Secret

Ho una ferita in cor che gitta sangue,
I-have a wound in heart that emits blood,
(I have a wound in my heart that bleeds,)

che a poco a poco mi farà morir.
that a little by little me will-make to-die.
(that little by little will make me die.)

Trafita dal dolor l'anima langue;
It-stings from-the sorrow the-soul languid;
(The languid soul stings from sorrow;)

amo e il segreto mio non posso dir.
I-love and the secret my not can to-say.
(I love and my secret cannot be spoken.)

Bello come la luce a me daccanto
Beautiful like the light to me near
(Sometimes I see my secret love near me)

il segreto amor mio veggo talor.
the secret love my I-see sometimes.
(beautiful like the light.)

Ei passa e sento in me come uno schianto,
He passes and I-feel in me like an affliction,
(He passes and, like an affliction, I feel in me)

un impeto di gioia e di dolor.
an impulse of joy and of sorrow.
(and impulse of joy and of sorrow.)

Dal primo giorno non ho mai sperato,
From-the first day not I-have ever hoped,
(From the first day I never hoped to have)

il segreto fatale ho chiuso in me.
the secret fatal I-have closed in me.
(the fatal secret closed within me.)

Ed egli non saprà d'esser amato,
And he not will-know of-being loved,
(And he will not know that he was loved,)

mi vedrà morta e non saprà perché.
me will-be dead and not will-know why.
(I will be dead and he will not know why.)

Eppur se il veggo, aprir vorrei le braccia,
And-yet if him I-see, to-open I-would-like the arms,
(And yet if I see him, I would like to open my arms,)

dirgli che l'amo e che il mio cor gli do.
to-tell-him that him-I-love and that the my heart him I-give.
(to tell him that I love him and that I give him my heart.)

Vorrei fissarlo arditamente in faccia,
I-would-like to-gaze-at-him ardently in face,
(I would like to gaze ardently into his face,)

Ma il cor mi trema e gli occhi alzar non so.
But the heart me trembles and the eyes to-raise not I-know.
(But my heart trembles and I do not know how to raise my eyes.)

Tosti
Si tu le voulais
If you it wanted

Si tu le voulais, ange aux yeux d'étoile,
If you it wanted, angel to-the eyes of-star,
(If you wanted, angel with the starry eyes,)

Je me reprendrais à vivre pour toi;
I me would-return to live for you;
(I would return to live for you;)

Mon coeur oublierait tout ce qui le voile
My heart would-forget all that which it veils
(My heart would forget all that which veils it)

Et j'aurais l'amour et j'aurais la foi.
And I-would-have the-love and I-will-have the faith.
(And I would have love and I will have faith.)

Si tu le voulais, mon âme à la tienne
If you it wanted, my soul to the yours
(If you wanted, my soul will carry the flower,)

Porterait sa fleur éclose pour toi;
It-would-carry its flower opened for you;
(opened for you, to your soul;)

Mon âme n'a rien qui ne t'appartienne;
My soul not-has nothing which not you-belongs;
(My soul has nothing which doesn't belong to you;)

Tu pourrais cuellir son rêve et sa foi.
You might-be-able to-gather its dream and its faith.
(You might be able to gather its dream and its faith.)

Si tu le voulais, je viendrais sourire
If you it wanted, I would-come to-smile
(If you wanted, I would come to smile)

A tous les moments tristes ou joyeux.
At all the moments sad or joyous.
(At all moments, sad or joyous.)

Je sais des chansons si douces à dire
I know of-the songs so sweet to tell
(I know songs so sweet to tell)

Pour percer l'esprit et fermer les yeux.
For piercing the-spirit and closing the eyes.
(For piercing the spirit and closing the eyes.)

Tosti
Sogno
Dream

Ho sognato che stavi a ginocchi
I-have dreamed that you-stay at knees
(I have dreamed that you are on your knees)

Come un santo che prega il Signior,
Like a saint who prays the Lord,
(Like a saint who prays to the Lord,)

Mi guardavi nel fondo degl'occhi,
Me you-did-gaze-at in-the depth of-the-eyes,
(You gazed at me and in the depth of your eyes,)

Sfavillava il tuo sguardo d'amor.
Sparkled the your glance of-love.
(Sparkled your glance of love.)

Tu parlavi e la voce sommessa
You did-speak and the voice low
(You spoke and your low voice)

Mi chiedea dolcemente mercè,
Me it-did-ask sweetly mercy,
(asked me sweetly for mercy,)

Solo un guardo che fosse promessa
Only a glance that is promised
(Only a glance that is promised)

Imploravi curvato al mio piè.
You-did-implore bended at-the my foot.
(Did you implore bended at my foot.)

Io taceva e coll'anima forte
I was-silent and with-the-soul strong
(I was silent and with my strong soul)

Il desio tentetore lottò,
The desire attempted I-struggled-for,
(I struggled for the attempted desire,)

Ho provato il martirio e la morte,
I-have felt the martydom and the death,
(I have felt martyrdom and death,)

pur mi vinsi e ti dissi di no.
yet me you-conquered and you said of no.
(yet me you conquered and said no.)

Ma il tuo labbro sfiorò la mia faccia
But the your lips touched the my face
(But your lips touched my face)

e la forza del cor mi tradì.
and the force of-the heart me betrayed.
(and the force of your heart betrayed me.)

Chiusi gli occhi, ti stesi le braccia,
You-closed the eyes, of-you stretched the arms,
(You closed your eyes, you stretched your arms,)

ma sognavo e il bel sogno svanì!
but I-was-dreaming and the beautiful dream vanished!
(but I was dreaming and the beautiful dream vanished!)

Tosti
Tormento
Torment

Quando ricorderò le tue carezze
When will-I-remember the your caresses
(Where will you be)

ove mai sarai tu?
where ever will-be you?
(when I remember your carresses?)

Di quei giorni di sogni e di dolcezze
Of those days of dreams and of sweetnesses
(Of those days of dreams and of sweetnesses)

che mai resterà più?
that never will-stay more?
(that will never be again?)

Quando ti chiamerò nel mio tormento
When you will-I-call in-the my torment
(Who will answer when I call you)

chi mai risponderà?
who ever it-will-answer?
(in my torment?)

Amore è come un'alito di vento: passa, carezza, va!
Love is like a-breath of wind: it-passes, it-caresses, it-goes!
(Love is like a breath of wind; it passes, it carresses, it goes!)

E se t'incontrerò su la mia via
And if you-I-will-meet on the my way
(And if I meet you on my way)

che mai dir ti potrò?
who ever to-say of-you will-be-able?
(who will be able to tell?)

Una stella filò come una scia e il mare la smorzò.
A star will-pour-out like a wave and the sea it will-quench.
(A star will pour out like a wave, and the sea will quench it.)

Ma s'io ti chiamerò come in quell'ore
But if-I you will-call like in those-hours
(But if I call you like in those hours,)

non fuggirmi così.
not to-flee-me like-this.
(don't flee from me like this.)

Non volgere la faccia al mio dolore se il tuo sogno mori!
Not to-turn the face to-the my sorrow if the your dream died!
(Don't turn your face to my sorrow if your dream dies!)

Tosti
Tristezza
Sadness

Guarda; lontan lontano muore ne l'onde il sol;
Look; far far-away dies of-it the-waves the sun;
(Look; far, far away the sun dies over the waves;)

stormi d'uccelli a vol tornano al piano.
you-rustle of-birds to fly back to-the plain.
(the birds rustle to fly back to the plain.)

Una malinconia io sento in cuore e pur non so perché;
A melancholy I feel in heart and yet not I-know why;
(I feel melancholy in my heart and yet I don't know why;)

guardondoti ne gli occhi, o bella mia,
look-they-to-you of-it the eyes, o beautiful-one my,
(My eyes look at you, o my beautiful one,)

muto mi stringo a te.
quiet me I-press to you.
(quietly I press myself to you.)

Copre l'ombria d'un manto le cose,
It-covers the-shadow of-a-cloak the things,
(The shadow of my cloak covers things,)

il cielo, il mar;
the heaven, the sea;
(the heaven, the sea;)

io sento tremolar ne gli occhi il pianto.
I feel trembling in the eyes the tears.
(I feel tears trembling in my eyes.)

Suona l'avemaria ed è si triste
It-sounds the-hail-mary and is so sad
(The Hail Mary sounds and is so sad)

e pur non so perché:
and yet not I-know why:
(and yet I don't know why:)

devotamente preghi, o bella mia,
devoutly you-pray, o beautiful-one my,
(devoutly you pray, o my beautiful one,)

io prego insiem con te.
I pray together with you.
(I pray together with you.)

Tenera ne la sera che s'empie di fulgor,
It-will-hold of-it the night that itself-fills of splendor,
(It will hold the night that fills itself with splendor,)

dai nostri amanti cuor va la preghiera.
of-the our lovers heart goes the prayer.
(The prayer goes to our lovers' hearts.)

E la malinconia mi fa pensare
And the melancholy me makes to-think
(And to think makes me melancholy)

e pur non so perché,
and yet not I-know why,
(and yet I don't know why,)

che un giorno ahimè, dovrà la vita mia
that one day alas, it-will-have the life my
(that one day, alas, my life will have)

perdere il sogno e te!
to-lose the dream and you!
(to lose the dream and you!)

Tosti
Vorrei
I-would-like

Vorrei, allor, che tu pallido e muto pieghi la fronte
I-would-like, then, that you pallid and mute bend the face
(I would like, then, that you, pallid and silent, to place your
face)

tra la fronte tra le mani e pensi
between the face between the hands and you-think
(between your hands and think)

e ti splendon
and of-you they-shine
(of the vain dreams of the)

su l'animo abbattuto i vani sogni
of the-soul killed the vain dreams
(killed soul which shine on you,)

ai desideri immensi, vorrei.
to-the desires immense, I-would-like.
(of their immense desires, I would like.)

Vorrei per incantesimi d'amore
I-would-like for spells of-love
(I would like for enchantments of love)

pianamente venire a 'l tuo richiamo, e ,
quietly to-come to the your recall, and,
(to come quietly to your memory, and,)

su di te piegando come un fiore,
on of you bending like a flower,
(bending toward you like a flower,)

con dolce voce susurrarti: Io t'amo!
with sweet voice whisper: I you-love!
(whisper with sweet voice: I love you!)

Vorrei di tutte le mie sciolte chiome cingerti
I-would-like of all the my free hairs to-enclose-you
(I would like all of my flowing hair to enclose you)

con lentissima carezza,
with very-slow caresses,
(with very slow caresses,)

e sentirmi da te chiamare a nome,
and to-feel-me of you to-call by name,
(and to feel you call me by name,)

vederti folle de la mia bellezza, vorrei.
to-see-you insane of the my beauty, I-would-like.
(to see you insane with my beauty, I would like.)

Tosti
Vorrei Morire!
I-would-like To-Die!

Vorrei morir ne la stagion dell'anno,
I-would-like to-die in the season of-the-year,
(I would like to die in the season of the year,)

Quando è tiepida l'aria e il ciel sereno,
When is warm the-air and the heaven serene,
(When the air is warm and the heaven serene,)

Quando le rondinelle il nido fanno,
When the swallows the nest make,
(When the swallows make their nests,)

Quando di nuovi fior s'orna il terreno;
When of new flowers themselves-adorn the earth;
(When new flowers adorn the earth;)

Vorrei morir quando tramonta il sole,
I-would-like to-die when sets the sun,
(I would like to die when the sun sets.)

Quando sul prato dormon le viole,
When on-the fields sleep the violets,
(When the violets sleep on the fields,)

Lieta farebbe a Dio l'alma ritorno
Glad could-make to God the-soul return
(Glad the soul could return to God,)

A primavera e sul morir del giorno.
To spring and on-the dying of-the day.
(To spring and to the dying of the day.)

Ma quando infuria il nembo e la tempesta,
But when enraged the cloud and the storm,
(But when the cloud and the storm are enraged,)

Allor che l'aria si fa scura scura:
Then that the-air so make dark dark:
(making, then, the air so dark, dark:)

Quando ai rami una foglia più non resta,
When to-the branches a leaf more not stays,
(When a leaf no longer stays on the branch,)

Allora di morire avrei paura.
Then of dying I-will-have fear.
(Then I will fear dying.)

Verdi
Ad una stella
To a star

Bell'astro della terra, Luce amorosa e bella, Beautiful-planet of-
the earth, Light loving and beautiful,
(Beautiful planet earth, loving and beautiful light,)

Come desia quest'anima Oppressa e prigioniera
How desires this-soul Oppressed and imprisoned
(How this soul, oppressed and imprisoned, desires)

Le sue catene infrangere, Libera a te volar!
The your chains to-break, Free to you to-fly!
(to break your chains, Free to fly to you!)

Gl'ignoti abitatori Che mi nascondi, o stella,
The-unknown inhabitants Who me you-hide, o star,
(O star, you hide me from the unknown inhabitants,)

Cogl'angeli s'abbracciano Puri fraterni amori,
With-the-angels they-embrace-us Pure brotherly loves,
(Pure brotherly love with the angels embrace us,)

Fan d'armonie cogl'angeli La sfera tua sonar.
Make of-harmony with-the-angels The sphere your to-sound.
(Make your sphere of sound join with the harmony of the
angels.)

Le colpe e i nostri affanni Vi sono a lor segreti,
The faults and the our pangs to-Them are to their secrets,
(Our faults and pangs are secret to them,)

Inavvertiti e placidi Scorrono i giorni
Unobserved and placid we-Run-through the days
(Unobserved and placid we run through our days)

e gli anni, Ne mai pensier li novera,
and the years, Neither never to-think the number,
(and years, Neither thinking of the number,)

Ne li richiama in duol.
Nor them recall in sorrow.
(nor recalling them in sorrow.)

Bell'astro della sera, Gemma che il cielo allieti,
Beautiful-star of-the night, Gem that the heaven enjoys,
(Beautiful star of the night, Gem in which the heavens delight,)

Come alzerà quest'anima Oppressa e prigioniera
How I-will-raise this-soul Oppressed and imprisoned
(How I will raise this oppressed and imprisoned soul)

Dal suo terreno carcere
From-the your earth imprisoned
(From your imprisoned earth)

Al tuo bel raggio il vol!
To-the your beautiful ray the flight!
(To the flight of your beautiful ray!)

Verdi
Ave Maria
Hail Mary

Ave regina...vergina Maria Piena di grazia:
Hail queen...virgin Mary Full of grace:
(Hail queen...virgin Mary Full of grace:)

Iddio e sempre teco: Sopra ogni donna benedetta sia.
God is always with-you: Above every woman blessed is.
(God is always with you: Above all women blessed.)

E'l frutto del tuo ventre, il qual io preco.
And-the fruit of-the your womb, the which I pray.
(And the fruit of your womb, of which I pray.)

Che ci guardi dal mal, Cristo Gesu, Sia benedetto,
That us guard from-the harm, Christ Jesus, Is blessed,
(That guards us from harm, Christ Jesus, Is blessed,)

e noi tiri con seco. Vergine benedetta, sempre tu...
and us draw with with-him. Virgin blessed, always you...
(and you draw us with you. Blessed Virgin, always you...)

Ora per noi a Dio, che ci perdoni, E diaci grazia
Hour for us to God, who us pardons, And give-us grace
(Our hour to God, who pardons us, And gives us grace)

a viver si quaggiù,
to live so down-here,
(to live thus down here,)

Che'l Paradiso al nostro fin di doni.
That-the Paradise to-the our last day you-give.
(That on our last day you will give us paradise.)

Brindisi - I & II
A Toast - I & II

Mescetemi il vino! Tu solo, o bicchiere,
Pour-me the wine! You alone, oh glass,
(Pour me the wine! You alone, oh glass,)

Fra gaudi terreni non sei menzognero,
Among joys earthly not know untruth,
(Among earthly joys know not untruth,)

Tu vita de' sensi, letizia del cor.
You life of-the senses, joy of-the heart.
(You life of the senses, joy of the heart.)

Amai; m'infiammaro due sguardi fatali;
I-loved; me-inflamed two glances fatal;
(I loved; two fatal eyes inflamed me;)

Credei l'amicizia fanciulla senz'ali,
I-believed the-friendship girl without-wings,
(I believed the friendship like a naive girl,)

Follia de' prim'anni, fantasma illusor.
Folly of first-years, phantasm deceptive.
(Folly of her young years, deceptive phantasm.)

Mescetemi il vino, letizia del cor.
Pour-me the wine, joy of-the heart.
(Pour me the wine, joy of my heart.)

L'amico, l'amante col tempo ne fugge,
The-friend, the-lover with-the time of-it flees,
(My friend, my lover flees with time,)

Ma tu non paventi chi tutto distrugge:
But you not fears he-who all destroys:
(But you do not fear he who destroys all:)

L'età non t'offende, t'accresce virtù.
The-age not you-offends, you-it-increases virtue.
(Age does not offend you, it increases your virtue.)

Sfiorito l'aprile, cadute le rose,
Fades the-April, fallen the roses,
(April has faded, the roses have fallen,)

Tu sei che n'allegri le cure noiose:
You know that of-it-happy the cares weary:
(You happily know its weary cares:)

Sei tu che ne torni la gioia che fu.
Know you that of-it return the joy that was.
(You know how to return to the joy that was.)

Mescetemi il vino, letizia del cor.
Pour-me the wine, joy of-the heart.
(Pour me the wine, joy of my heart.)

Chi meglio risana del cor le ferite?
Who better heals of-the heart the wounds?
(Who better heals the wounds of the heart?)

Se te non ci desse la provvida vite,
If of-you not here gives the provident vineyards,
(Here if you did not give the good vineyards,)

Sarebbe immortale l'umano dolor.
Might-be immortal the-human sorrow.
(human sorrow might me immortal.)

Deh, pietoso, oh Addolorata
Oh, pitious, oh Our-Lady-of-Sorrows

Deh, pietoso, oh Addolorata, China il guardo Oh, pitious, oh
Our-Lady-of-Sorrows, Bend the glance
(Oh, pitious, oh Our Lady of Sorrows, bend your glance)

al mio dolore; Tu, una spada fitta in core,
to-the my sorrow; You, a sword fixed in heart,
(to my sorrow; You, a sword fixed in your heart,)

Volgi gl'occhi desolata Al morente tuo figliuol.
Turn the-eyes afflicted To-the dying your son.
(To your dying son turn your afflicted eyes.)

Quelle occhiate, i sospir vanno Lassù al padre
Those glances, the sighs go Up-there to-the father
(Those glances and sighs which are his vigor and his anxiety)

e son preghiere Che il suo tempri ed il tuo affanno.
and are prayer That the his vigor and the his anxiety.
(go up to the father and are a prayer.)

Come a me squarcin le viscere Gl'insoffribili miei guai
Like to me tear the organs The-intolorable my woes
(Like my intolorable woes tear my organs)

E dell'ansio petto i palpiti
And of-the-anxious breast the palpitations
(Who can ever comprehend the palpitations)

Chi comprendere può mai?
Who comprehends can ever?
(of my anxious breast?)

Di che trema il cor? Che vuol?
Of that trembles the heart? That you-want?
(The heart trembles from that? Do you want that?)

Ah! tu sola il sai, tu sol!
Ah! you alone it know, you alone!
(Ah! only you know it, only you!)

Sempre, ovunque il passo io giro, Qual martiro,
Always, everywhere the step I look, What martyrdom,
(Always, everywhere I step I look, What martyrdom,)

qual martiro Qui nel sen porto con me!
what martyrdom Here in-the breast I-carry with me!
(what martyrdom I carry with me here in my breast!)

Solitaria appena, ho, quanto Verso allora,
Solitary scarcely, I-have, how-much I-pour-out then,
(Scarcely alone, I am, how much pouring out then,)

oh quanto pianto E di dentro scoppia il cor.
oh how-much crying And of within bursts the heart.
(oh how much crying And inside my heart bursts.)

Sul vasel del finestrino La mia lacrima scendea
On-the vessel of-the small-window The my tear fell
(On the vase at the small window my tear fell)

Quando all'alba del mattino
When at-the-dawn of-the morning
(When at this morning's dawn)

Questi fior per te cogliea,
These flowers for you gathered,
(I gathered these flowers for you,)

Chè del sole il primo raggio La mia stanza rischiarava
That of-the sun the first ray The my room brightens
(That at the first ray of the sun my room brightens)

E dal letto mi cacciava Agitandomi il dolor.
And of-the bed me it-intrudes Agitating-me the sorrow.
(And intrudes my bed, agitating my sorrow.)

Ah, per te dal disonore, Dalla morte io sia salvata.
Ah, for you of-the shame, From-the death I am saved.
(Ah, of shame for you, I am saved from death.)

Il mistero
The mystery

Se tranquillo a te d'accanto, Donna mia, talun mi vede,
If tranquil to you near-by, Lady my, someone me sees,
(If, my Lady, someone sees me tranquil near you,)

O felice appien mi crede O guarito dall'amor; Oh happiness
complete me believe Oh healer of-the-love;
(Believe me, Oh healer of love, Oh happiness complete;)

Ma non tu, che sai pur quanto
But not you, who knows still how-much
(But not you, who still knows how much)

Combattuto e oppresso ho il cor.
Struggle and oppression I-have in heart.
(struggle and oppression I have in my heart.)

Come lago, che stagnante Par che dorma e appena mouva,
Like lake, that stagnate For that sleeps and hardly moves,
(Like a lake, that stagnate, sleeps and hardly moves,)

Ma tempeste in fondo cova Sconosciute al vïator,
But tempest in bottom broods Unknown to-the traveller,
(in the bottom broods a storm unknown to the traveller,)

Ma tal calma ho nel sembiante, Ho scompiglio,
But such calm I-have in-the appearance, I-have confusion,
(Ah I have such calm in my appearance, I have confusion)

ho in fondo al cor.
I-have in bottom to-the heart.
(in the bottom of my heart.)

Se un sospiro, se un lamento Il timore a me contende,
If a sigh, if a groan That fear to me prevents,
(If fear prevents me a sigh or a groan,)

Del timore che m'accende
Of-the fear that me-burns
(I will not lessen the intense ardor)

Non scemò l'intenso ardor.
Not I-will-lessen the-intense ardor.
(of the fear that burns me.)

Come lampa in monumento Non veduto avvampa in cor
Like lamp in monument Not seen blazes in heart
(My heart blazes like the unseen lamp in a monument)

E vivrà benchè respresso, Benchè privo di conforto
And will-live although repressed, Although devoid of comfort
(And will live although repressed and devoid of comfort)

E vivrebbe ancor che morto Lo volesse il tuo rigor.
And will-live still that dead It wants the your severity.
(and will still live, dead it wants your severity.)

Chè alimento da sè stesso Prende amore in nobil cor.
Because food from it itself Takes love in noble heart.
(Because love in a noble heart takes food from itself.)

Il poveretto
The poor-little-one

Passegger, che al dolce aspetto
Passer-by, who to-the sweet appearance
(Passerby, with the sweet appearance)

Par che serbi un gentil cor,
For that you-keep a gentle heart,
(of a gentle heart,)

Porgi un soldo al poveretto
Pour a penny to-the poor-one
(Give a penny to the poor one)

Che da man digiuno è ancor.
Who by hand begging is still.
(Who is still begging.)

Fin da quando ero figliuolo Sono stato militar
Until of when was son I-have been soldier
(I have been a soldier until I had a son)

E pugnando pel mio suolo
And fighting for-the my soul
(And fighting for my soul)

Ho trascorso e terra e mar;
I-have traversed and earth and sea;
(I have traversed earth and sea;)

Ma or che il tempo su me pesa,
But know that the time on me weighs,
(But now that time weighs on me,)

Or che forza più non ho,
Now that force more not I-have,
(Now that I am no longer strong,)

Fin la terra che ho difesa,
Until the.earth that I-have defended,
(Until now the earth which I have defended,)

La mia patria m'oblio.
The my fatherland me-forgets.
(My country has forgotten me.)

Il tramonto
The sunset

Amo l'ora del giorno che muore Quando il sole I-love the-hour
of-the day that dies When the sun
(I love the hour of the day that dies when the sun,)

già stanco declina, E nell'onde di queta marina
already tired sets, And in-the-waves of quiet marina
(already tired, sets, And in the waves of the quiet marina)

Veggo il raggio supremo lanquir.
I-see the ray highest lanquish.
(I see the highest ray languish.)

In quell'ora mi torna nel core
In that-hour me returns in-the heart
(In that hour in my heart returns)

Un'età più felice di questa;
An-age more happy of this;
(An age happier than this;)

In quell'ora dolcissima e mesta Volgo a te,
In that-hour very-sweet and sad I-turn to you,
(In that very sweet and sad hour I turn to you,)

cara donna, il sospir.
dear lady, the sigh.
(dear lady, my sigh.)

L'occhio immoto ed immoto il pensiero,
The-eye motionless and motionless the thought,
(My eyes motionless and motionless my thought,)

Io contemplo la striscia lucente
I contemplate the streak shining
(I contemplate the shining streak)

Che mi vien dal seren,
That me comes of-the serene,
(That comes to me from the serene,)

dal sereno occidente La quiete solcando, solcando del mar.
of-the serene west The quiet plowing, plowing of-the sea.
(from the serene west The quiet plowing, plowing of the sea.)

E desio di quell'aureo sentiero
And I-desire of that-gold path
(And I desire that gold path)

Ravviarmi sull'orma infinita Quasi debba la stanca
Restarts-me on-the-trace infinite Like must the tired
(And starts me again on the infinite trail Like guides)

mia vita Ad un porto di pace guidar.
my life To a port of peace to-guide.
(my tired life to a port of peace.)

In solitaria stanza
In solitary room

In solitaria stanza Langue per doglia atroce;
In solitary room he-Languishes of pain atrocious;
(In a solitary room he languishes with atrocious pain;)

Il labbro è senza voce, Senza respiro il sen, The lip is without
voice, Without breath the breast,
(his lips are voiceless, his breast breathless,)

Come in deserta aiuola, Che di rugiade è priva,
Like in deserted flower-bed, That of dew is deprived,
(Like in the deserted flower-bed, deprived of dew,)

Sotto alla vampa estiva Molle narciso svien. Under to-the blaze
summer Delicate narcissus grow.
(Under the hot summer sun delicate narcissus grow.)

Io, dall'affanno oppresso, Corro per vie rimote
I, of-the-desire oppressed, I-run for life remote
(I, with oppressed desire, run for a remote life)

E grido in suon che puote Le rupi intenerir
And I-scream in sound that could The rocks to-effect
(And scream in a voice that could save the rocks,)

Salvate, o Dei pietosi, Quella beltà celeste;   to-Save, oh God
pitious, That beauty heavenly;
(oh pitious God, that heavenly beauty;)

Voi forse non sapreste Un'altra Irene ordir.
You perhaps not might-know Another Irene to-intrigue.
(You may not know another Irene to intrigue.)

Verdi
L'esule
The-exiled-one

Vedi! la bianca luna Splende sui colli;
Look! the white moon Shines on-the hills;
(Look! the white moon shines on the hills;)

la notturna brezza Scorre leggera ad increspare
the nightly breeze Runs light to-the ripple
(the evening breeze runs lightly rippling)

il vago Grembo del queto lago.
the pretty Tomb of-the calm lake.
(the pretty tomb of the calm lake.)

Perchè sol io Nell'ora più tranquilla e più soave
Why alone I In-the-hour more tranquil and more sweet
(Why I alone in an hour more tranquil and sweeter)

Muto e pensoso mi starò? Qui tutto E gioia;
Silent and thoughtful me I-will-remain? Here all Is joy;
(Silent and thoughtful I will remain? Here all is joy;)

il ciel, la terra Di natura sorridono all'incanto.
the heaven, the earth Of nature smile at-the enchantment.
(nature's heaven and earth smile at the enchantment.)

L'esule solo è condannato al pianto.
The-refugee alone is condemned to-the weeping.
(The lone refugee is condemned to weeping.)

Ed io pure fra l'aure native
And I still among the-breezes native
(And still I among the native breezes)

Palpitava d'ignoto piacer.
Palpitate of-unknown pleasure.
(Palpitate of unknown pleasure.)

Oh, del tempo felice ancor vive
Oh, of-the time happy still lives
(Oh, the warm thought of a happy time)

La memoria nel caldo pensier.
The memory in-the warm thought.
(still lives in my memory.)

Corsi lande, deserti, foreste,
I-ran-through moors, deserts, forests,
(I ran through moors, deserts, forests,)

Vidi luoghi olezzanti di fior;
I-saw places fragrant of flower;
(I saw places fragrant with flowers;)

M'aggirai fra le danze e le feste,
Me-turned-around among the dances and the festivals,
(I turned among the dances and festivals,)

Ma compagno ebbi sempre il dolor.
But companion I-was always the sorrow.
(But I was always the companion of sorrow.)

Or che mi resta?...togliere alla vita
Now that me stay?...to-take-away to-the life
(Now I should stay thus?...to be taken to a life)

Quella forza che misero mi fa.
That force that miserable me makes.
(that forces me to be miserable.)

Deh, vieni, vieni, o morte, a chi t'invita
Oh, come, come, oh death, to who you-invites
(Oh, come, come, oh death, to him who invites you)

E l'alma ai primi gaudi tornerà.
And the-soul to-the first joys will-return.
(And the soul of my first joys will return.)

Oh, che allor le patrie sponde Non saranno a me vietate;
Oh, what then the native banks Not will-be to me forbidden;
(Oh, then the native banks will not be forbidden to me;)

Fra quell'aure, su quell'onde
Among those-breezes, on those-waves
(Among those breezes, on those waves)

Nudo spirto volerò;
Unadorned spirit will-fly;
(my unadorned spirit will fly;)

Bacerò le guance amate Della cara genitrice
I-will-kiss the cheeks loving Of-the dear mother
(I will kiss the loving cheeks of my dear mother)

Ed il pianto all'infelice Non veduto tergerò,
And the tears to-the-unhappy Not seen I-will-dry,
(And the tears of the unseen unhappy ones I will dry,)

Ed il pianto, il pianto all'infelice tergerò.
And the tears, the tears to-the-unhappy I-will-dry.
(And the tears, the tears of the unhappy I will dry.)

La seduzione
The seduction

Era bella com'angiol del cielo,
Was beautiful like-an-angel of-the heavens,
(She was beautiful like a heavenly angel,)

Innocente degl'anni sul fiore,
Innocent of-the-years in-the flower,
(Innocent as the flowering of a new year,)

Ed il palpito primo d'amore
And the palpitations first of-love
(And with the first palpitations of love)

Un crudele nel cor le destò.
A cruel-one in-the heart them will-awake.
(A cruel one in her heart will awake them.)

Inesperta, fidente ne' giuri,
Inexperienced, trustful in-the oaths,
(Inexperienced, trusting of oaths,)

Sè commise all'amante sleale;
Herself she-pities to-the-lover disloyal;
(She herself pities the disloyal lover;)

Fu sedotta! e l'anello nuziale, Poveretta,
Was seduced! and the-ring nuptial, Poor-little-one,
(She was seduced! and her wedding ring, Poor-little-one,)

ma indarno invoco. All'infamia dannata,
but invain invoked. To-the-shame damned,
(invoked invain. To shame damned,)

allo scherno, Nove lune gemè la tradita;
to-the scorn, Nine moons lament the betrayed-one;
(to scorn, nine months lament the betrayed one;)

Poi, consunta dal duolo la vita,
Then, consumed of-the sorrow the life,
(Then, consumed in the sorrow of life,)

Pregò venia al crudele e spirò.
I-will-pray pardons to-the cruel-one and I-will-die.
(I will pray for pardon to the cruel one and will die.)

Ed il frutto del vil tradimento
And the fruit of-the vile betrayal
(And the fruit of the vile betrayal)

Nel sepolcro posogli d'appresso;
In-the grave lay-him of-near;
(Near in the grave lay him;)

Là non sorse una croce, un cipresso,
There not rose a cross, a cypress,
(There a cross is not erected, nor a cypress,)

Non un sasso il suo nome portò.
Not a stone the your name will-bear.
(Not a stone will bear your name.)

La zingara
The gypsy

Chi padre mi fosse qual patria mi sia,
Who father me was which native me is,
(Which father is my native one,)

Invano la gente chiamando mi va;
Invain the people calling me go;
(Invain the people name me;)

Del primo mai seppi ed è patria mia
Of-the first never I-know and is native my
(Of that I shall never know my native land)

La terra che un fiore, che un frutto mi dà.
The land that a flower, that a fruit me gave.
(is that of a flower, which a fruit gave me.)

Dovunque il destino m'addita un sentiero,
Everywhere the destiny me-it-shows a path,
(Everywhere destiny shows me a path,)

Io trovo un sorriso, io trovo un amor;
I find a smile, I find a love;
(I find a smile, I find a love;)

Perchè del passato darommi pensiero,
Why of-the past will-give-me thought,
(Why should the past give me thought,)

se l'ora presente è lieta al mio cor?
if the-hour present is joyful to-the my heart?
(if the present hour is joyful to my heart?)

Può, è vero, il domani un torbido velo
Can, is true, the tomorrow a troubled veil
(Tomorrow may, it's true, bring a troubled veil)

Dell'aure serene l'aspetto turbar;
Of-the-breezes serene the-image to-trouble;
(to my image of serene breezes;)

Ma s'oggi risplende azzurro il mio cielo,
But if-today shines blue the my heaven,
(But, if my heaven shines blue today,)

Perchè rattristarmi d'un dubbio avvenir?
Why grieve-me of-a doubtful future?
(Why grieve of a doubtful future?)

Io sono una pianta che ghiaccio non spoglia,
I am a plant that frost not spoils,
(I am a plant that frost does not spoil,)

Che tutto disfida del verno il rigor;
That all challenges of-the winter the severity;
(That winter challenges with its severity;)

Se fronda qui cade, la un'altra germoglia,
If leafy here falls, there another sprout,
(If a leaf falls here, there another will sprout,)

In ogni stagione son carca di fior.
In every season is laden of flowers.
(every season is laden with flowers.)

Lo spazzacimino
The chimney-sweep

Lo spazzacamin! Son d'aspetto brutto e nero,
The chimney-sweep! I-am of-appearance ugly and black,
(The chimney-sweep! I am ugly and black in appearance,)

Tingo ognun che mi vien presso;
I-stain everyone who me comes near;
(I stain everyone who comes near me;)

Sono d'abiti mal messo,
I-am of-clothes badly dressed,
(I am badly dressed,)

Sempre scalzo intorno io vo.
Always barefooted around I go.
(I always go around barefooted.)

Ah! di me chi sia più lieto
Ah! of me who is more happy
(Ah! to me one who is more happy)

Sulla terra dir non so. Spazzacamin!
On-the earth to-say not I-know. Chimney-sweep!
(On earth I do not know. Chimney-sweep!)

Signori, signore, lo spazzacamin
Gentlemen, ladies, the chimney-sweep
(Gentlemen, ladies, you save the chimney-sweep)

Vi salva dal fuoco per pochi quattrin.
You save from-the fire for little farthing.
(from the fire for a few farthings.)

Ah! Io mi levo innanzi al sole E di tutta la cittade
Ah! I me rise before to-the sun And of all the city
(Ah! I rise before the sun and go all about the streets)

Col mio grido empio le strade
With-the my shout heathen the streets
(of the city with my heathen shouts)

E nemico alcun non ho.
And enemy any not I-have.
(and have not one enemy.)

Ah! di me chi sia più lieto
Ah! of me who is more happy-know.
(Ah! to me one who is more happy)

Sulla terra dir non so.
On-the earth to-say not I
(on earth I do not know.)

Talor m'alzo sovra i tetti,
Sometimes me-see on the roofs,
(Sometimes you see me on the roofs,)

Talor vado per le sale;
Sometimes I-go for the rooms;
(Sometimes in the rooms;)

Col mio nome i fanciuletti Timorosi e quieti io fo.
With-the my name the little-boys Timid and quiet I make.
(With my name I make the little boys timid and quiet.)

Ah! di me chi sia più lieto
Ah! of me who is more happy
(Ah! to me one who is more happy)

Sulla terra dir non so.
On-the earth to say-not I-know.
(on earth I do not know.)

More, Elisa, lo stanco poeta
Dies, Elisa, the tired poet

More, Elisa, lo stanco poeta E l'estremo origlier
Dies, Elisa, the tired poet And the-last pillow
(The tired poet dies, Elisa, and the last pillow)

su cui more É quell'arpa che un tempo l'amore
under whom dies Is that-harp that one time the-love
(under him who dies is that harp which at one time)

Insegnava al suo spirto gentil.
Taught to-the your spirit gentle.
(Taught your gentle spirit love.)

More pago che pura risplenda
Dies satisfied that purity shines
(Dies satisfied that purity shines)

Come quella d'un angiol del cielo;
Like that of-an angel of-the heaven;
(Like that of a heavenly angel;)

Giacerà senza frale e uno stelo
He-will-lie-down without frailty and a stem
(He will lie down without frailty and a stem)

Fiorirà tra le corde d'april.
Will-flower among the ropes of-April.
(Will flower among the rains of April.)

Dono estremo, per te lo raccogli
Gift last, for you it gather
(This last gift, for you to gather)

Senza insano dolor, senza pianto;
Without insane sorrow, without tears;
(Without insane sorrow, without tears.)

Una lacrima cara soltanto, Solo un vale che gema fedel.
One tear dear only, Alone a farewell that laments faithful.
(One dear tear only, that faithfully laments alone.)

Che quest'alma già lascia le care Feste,
That this-soul already leaves the dear Rejoicings,
(That this soul already leaves the dear rejoicings,)

i canti le danze, gli amori,
the songs the dances, the loves,
(the songs the dances, the loves,)

Come un'aura che uscendo dai fiori
Like a-gentle-breeze that emerging from-the flowers
(Like a gentle breeze that emerging from the fragrant)

Odorosa s'effonda nel ciel.
Fragrant pours-out in-the heaven.
(Flowers pours out into the heavens.)

Nell'orror di notte oscura
In-the-horror of night dark

Nell'orror di notte oscura, Quando tace il mondo intier,
In-the-horror of night dark, When silent the world entire,
(In the horror of the dark night, When the entire world is silent,)

Del mio bene in fra le mura
Of-the my beloved in among the walls
(Within the walls fly the thoughts)

Vola sempre il mio pensier.
Fly always the my thought.
(of my beloved.)

E colei che tanto adoro
And she who so-much I-adore
(And perhaps the wall will surround)

Forse ad altri il cordonò;
Perhaps to-the others it will-surround.
(she who I so much adore.)

Ciel, per me non v'ha ristoro, Io d'ambascia morirò.
Heaven, for me not you-it-has restored, I of-agony will-die.
(Heaven has not restored you for me, I will die of agony.)

Quando in terra il giorno imbruna Il mio spirto apparirà
When in earth the day darkens The my spirit will-appear
(My spirit will appear when the day darkens on earth)

Ed il raggio della luna fosco si vedrà.
And the ray of-the moon dark so will-see.
(And the dark ray of the moon thus will see.)

D'un amante moribondo, D'un tradito adorator,
Of-a lover dying, Of-a traitor adored,
(The entire world will hear the sorrowful lament,)

Udirà l'intero mondo Il lamento del dolor.
It-will-hear the-entire world The lament of-the sorrow.
(Of a dying lover, Of an adored traitor.)

E d'amore nella storia Sarà scritto ognor così:
And of-love in-the story Will-be written always like-this:
(And the story of love will be always written like this:)

Maledetta la memoria Di colei che lo tradì!
Curse the memory Of she who him betrayed!
(Of she who betrayed him, curse the memory!)

Non t'accostare all'urna
Not you-approach to-the tomb

Non t'accostare all'urna Che il cener mio rinserra;
Not you-approach to-the urn That the ashes my will-contain;
(Do not approach the urn which will contain my ashes;)

Questa pietosa terra E sacra al mio dolor.
This pitious earth Is sacred to-the my sorrow.
(This pitious soil is sacred to my sorrow.)

Odio gli affanni tuoi, Ricuso i tuoi giacinti; I-hate the pangs
your, I-refuse the your hyacinths;
(I hate your anguish, I refuse your hyacinths;)

Che giovano agli estinti Due lacrime o due fior?
That young to-the dead Two tears or two flowers?
(That recently dead Two tears or two flowers?)

Empia! dovevi allora Porgermi un fil d'aita
Wicked-one! where-you then To-offer-me a line of-help
(Wicked one! do you now offer me help)

Quando traea la vita Nell'ansia e nei sospir. When it-brought the
life In-the-anxiety and in-the sighing.
(When it-brought life to your anxiety and to your sighing.)

A che d'inutil pianto Assordi la foresta?
To whom of-useless tear Deafen the forest?
(To whom do you deafen the forest with your useless tear?)

Rispetta un'ombra mesta E lasciala dormir.
(Respect a-shadow sad And let-it sleep.)
(Respect a sad shadow and let it sleep.)

Verdi
Perduta ho la pace
Lost I-have the peace

Perduta ho la pace, ho in cor mille guai;
Lost I-have the peace, I-have in heart 1000 woes;
(I have lost peace, I have in my heart 1000 woes;)

Ah, no, più non spero trovarla più mai.
Ah, no, more not I-hope to-find-it more never.
(Ah, no, I can hope to find it never again.)

M'è buio di tomba ov'egli non è;
Me-has darkness of tomb where-he not is;
(Everywhere he is not is like a tomb;)

Senz'esso un deserto è il mondo per me.
Without-him a desert is the world for me.
(Without him the world is a desert for me.)

Mio povero capo confuso travolto;
My poor head confused upset;
(My poor head is confused, upset;)

Oh misera, il senno, il senno m'è tolto!
Oh misery, the sense, the sense to-me-is removed!
(Oh misery, my senses, my senses are gone!)

S'io sto al finestrello, ho gl'occhi a lui solo;
If-I stay at-the window, I-have the-eyes for him alone;
(If I stay at the window, I watch for him alone;)

S'io sfuggo di casa, sol dietro a lui volo.
If-I escape from house, only back to him I-fly.
(If I leave the house, only back to him I fly.)

Oh, il bel portamento; oh, il vago suo viso!
Oh, the beautiful bearing; oh, the beautiful his visage!
(Oh, his beautiful bearing; oh, his beautiful face!)

Qual forza è nei sguardi, che dolce sorriso!
What force is in-the glances, what sweet smile!
(What force is in his glances, what a sweet smile!)

E son le parole un magico rio;
And are the words a magic brook;
(And his words are a magic brook;)

Qual stringer di mano, qual bacio, mio Dio!
What to-clasp of hand, what kiss, my God!
(What a clasp of his hand, what a kiss, my God!)

Anela congiungersi al suo il mio petto;
Breathless to-join to-the his the my breast;
(Breathless to join his breast to mine;)

Potessi abbracciarlo, tenerlo a me stretto!
I-could embrace-him, hold-him to me tight!
(I could embrace him, hold him to me tightly!)

Baciarlo potessi, far pago il desir!
To-kiss-him I-could, make satisfied the desire!
(I could kiss him, to satisfy my desire!)

Baciarlo! e potessi baciata morir.
To-kiss-him! and I-could kissed to-die.
(To kiss him! and I could, being kissed, die.)

Verdi
Stornello
Little Song

Tu dici che non m'ami...anch'io non t'amo...
You say that not me-you-love...also-I not you-love...
(You say that you don't love me...I don't love you either...)

Dici non mi vuoi ben, non te ne voglio.
You-say not me you-wish well, not you neither I-want.
(You say that you don't love me, I don't love you either.)

Dici ch'a un altro pesce hai teso l'amo.
You-say that-you-have an other fish you-have tight it-I-love.
(You say that you have caught another fish.)

Anch'io in altro giardin la rosa coglio.
Also-I in another garden the rose I-gather.
(I gather roses in another garden too.)

Anco di questo vo'che ci accordiamo:
Also of this I-want-that us we-agree:
(Also on this I want us to agree:)

Tu fa quel che ti pare, io quel che voglio.
You do that which you think, I that which I-want.
(You do what you wish, and I'll do what I wish.)

Son libera di me, padrone è ognuno.
I-am free of myself, master is each-one.
(I am myself free, everyone is a master.)

Serva di tutti e non servo a nessuno.
Servant of all and not I-serve to no-one.
(I'm of service to all and servant to no one.)

Costanza nell'amor è una follia;
Constancy in-the-love is a folly;
(Constancy in love is folly;)

Volubile io sono e me ne vanto.
Inconstant I am and me of-it I-brag.
(I am inconstant and I brag about it.)

Non tremo più scontrandoti per via,
Not I-tremble more to-encounter-you on street,
(I don't tremble to see you on the street,)

Nè, quando sei lontan mi struggo in pianto.
Nor, when you-are far-away me I-pine-away in tears.
(Nor, when you're far away do I pine away in tears.)

Come usignol che uscì di prigionia
Like nightingale who emerges from prison
(Like the nightingale who emerges from prison)

Tutta la notte e il dì folleggio e canto.
All the night and the day I-frolic and I-sing.
(All day and night I frolic and sing.)